A Smarter Way to
Learn Pool

A Smarter Way to Learn Pool

PROVEN TECHNIQUES FOR MASTERING THE GAME

GEORGE FELS

CB

CONTEMPORARY BOOKS

Library of Congress Cataloging-in-Publication Data

Fels, George.
    A smarter way to learn pool : proven techniques for mastering
the game / George Fels.
      p.   cm.
    ISBN 0-8092-2849-1
    1. Pool (Game)   2. Pool (Game)—Psychological aspects.
I. Title.
GV891.F42   1999
794.7'3—dc21
                                            98-38852
                                              CIP

Cover photograph copyright © 1996 Tom and DeeAnn McCarthy/The Stock Market
Cover design by Scott Rattray
Interior design by Amy Yu Ng
Interior photography by John Parris Frantz, JPF Associates Communications, Chicago

Published by Contemporary Books
A division of NTC/Contemporary Publishing Group, Inc.
4255 West Touhy Avenue, Lincolnwood (Chicago), Illinois 60646-1975 U.S.A.
Printed in the United States of America
International Standard Book Number: 0-8092-2849-1

99 00 01 02 03 QP 19 18 17 16 15 14 13 12 11 10 9 8 7 6 5 4 3 2 1

This book is dedicated to Dale Fels, who forgave all my basic flaws in the pool game of life.

CONTENTS

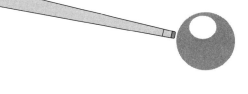

Introduction

Why This Pool Book Is Different

As a product (or perhaps *survivor* says it better) of the Chicago Public Schools, I learned many moons ago that there is such a thing as an excess of correctness.

What I mean by that is, to memorize a correct answer—to memorize anything, really—is not nearly the same thing as *learning* it. Once you understand *why* something is correct or incorrect, you're far closer to having learned it than someone who merely parrots back the correct answer by rote. It's quite possible, of course, to go through life doing everything as you were originally taught it should be correctly done. But that would clearly make for consistent underachievement, to say nothing of being boring as hell.

I'm willing to assume this is not the first pool book you have examined, however closely. By now you probably know that the great majority of pool books, especially those dealing with fundamentals, are simplistic, repetitive, and of only limited help. It's not necessarily that their information is out-and-out wrong; it's simply that the authors don't go far enough to offer you insights into what you're doing, and pool is largely a mental game. Skim the surface by following their instructions to the letter, and I can practically guarantee that you will never even approach your pool potential.

Let's consider an example from another sport. It's widely agreed that the most difficult thing to do in all of sports is hit a well-pitched fastball. If it's that hard (and it is), wouldn't you expect a hard-and-fast set of instructions as to how to go about it?

Yet among all the 700 or so major-league players, you will rarely find two identical stances or swings. Sure, the best hitters follow the same guidelines; they keep their heads still, they don't drop their hands, they stride into the pitch, and so forth. But look at all the different ways they execute and still get the job done.

If you're serious about learning pool, and especially learning it in a way that gives you a reasonable chance of playing it well, my hunch is that you'll do better with a book that examines what you do plus why you do it that way, and what your options are, in some depth. This is that book. I will pass along what I know in the same spirit in which I would like to have been taught (but wasn't, either in public school or in pool).

Your part of the bargain is to get to the table and practice what I say. The very best pool is played by intuition, not analysis, and you'll simply never develop your intuitive abilities any other way than by playing. There are some super books on advanced play (including mine); there are some good pool videos; there's even a wall chart (I know; I wrote that, too). But no one's words, mine or anyone else's, are going to make you into a player. Almost every other pool book, for instance, offers you generally correct instruction for forming the loop (professional) bridge. But almost none tells you that you'll never get comfortable with that bridge unless you play at least once a week, hopefully more. It's too unnatural a position for the fingers otherwise.

That's how we'll approach things here, taking you through the basics a bit more analytically and in a bit more depth, and continuing into your perspectives on practice (the right kind) and the three major forms of pool. What I hope to convey to you are the proper tools—not rules—to build the nucleus of a sound pool game.

One final bit of advice, definitely wise but not necessarily easy to heed: *No matter how eager you are to see your pool game improve, don't try to learn too much at once.* A recent study at Johns Hopkins University concluded that after learning a new athletic skill, the human brain needs approximately six hours to store the memory permanently—and if the process of storing that memory is interrupted by the process of learning another new skill, the memory of the first skill will be erased. Yes, eventually you must combine all the details of proper pool basics to execute correctly. But be patient, and assign yourself realistic goals. Some beginners progress far more quickly than others, having largely to do with natural talent. Go at your own pace, not somebody else's, and remember that the main idea of pool, as with any game, is to have fun.

Welcome to the world's greatest game—and, as you might expect, it only gets greater as you play it better. Let's get started.

THE BASICS—AND WHAT YOU'RE NOT USUALLY TAUGHT ABOUT THEM

Your Body

Why begin here? Because for all the talk you hear about "cue-ball control," that phrase is actually something of a misnomer. No matter how brilliant a pool genius you are destined to be, you will never, ever achieve anything more than *partial* control over the cue ball (and no control whatsoever over the object balls, despite all the twisting, leaping, steering, bellowing, and grimacing you see among players who are still willing to try; there's even a mythic story about a player who got so worked up in his "body English" that he backed through a second-story window).

What you potentially have *total* control over, however, are your body and your cue. That's what you should strive for; and it's even worth practicing, if briefly, in the absence of any balls on the table, especially while you're still getting comfortable with your stance and your stroke. No matter how intimidating pool shotmaking may appear at first, you have my personal guarantee that everything will fall into place quite naturally if you'll just control your body and your cue.

Am I making this sound easier than it is? Yes. A correct pool stroke is so simple that hardly anyone can do it. Nothing is really supposed to move except your stroking forearm and your eyeballs, and yet you'll see bobbing heads, weaving torsos, and upper-arm movement all over the place, possibly even among some fairly accomplished players. Everybody seems to want to add something extraneous; that's what makes body control so critical.

Does your body type affect your pool potential? Not likely. Today's top echelon of male players presents all shapes and sizes, including obesity. Physical strength is no factor whatsoever, and is probably not even desirable. Nevertheless, while this isn't *Muscle & Fitness* magazine, you should understand that being in reasonably good shape cannot possibly hurt your pool game, and could very well help. Not only would you be more comfortable in your shooting stance, and be far more easily able to play longer sessions, but you would enjoy the sound mind that comes with a sound body; and remember, pool is mostly mental.

If you already exercise regularly, or if you're dedicated enough to pool that you're willing to train for it, my recommendation would be aerobic, rather than anaerobic, exercise (that is, walking, jogging, biking, aerobics, and so on, instead of strength drills such as weightlifting). What you're after is a pair of well-toned legs and a reasonably flat abdomen; the latter ensures that your back won't have to work overtime as you get older, and you want to be good friends with your back if you want to play a lot of pool. Personally, I've been an iron-pumper for 40 years, but besides keeping my body firm and possibly keeping me mentally tough too, I doubt weightlifting has contributed much to my pool game. The essence of muscularity is feeling tight; the essence of pool playing is feeling loose, and never the twain shall meet. (To this day, it takes me a bare minimum of 20 minutes' practice before I feel loose enough to play.) Most of today's best pool players are pretty fair athletes—after all, pool is nothing more physically than hand–eye coordination, the basis of all sports—but only rarely will any sport a hint of real muscle.

A personal theory of mine is that martial arts training would be a terrific adjunct to your pool playing. Not only is it a great conditioner, but it offers you the chance to develop your confidence, mental calm, hand speed (necessary to maximize your break in 8-ball and 9-ball), and most of all, your powers of *focus*. That last aspect is absolutely critical to successful pool.

What is it you'll be asking your body to do, that we're giving it this kind of attention? Largely, to be on your feet for extended periods of time, and to bend forward and straighten up again many times over. It sounds like child's play to read about, and only a senior citizen would look at pool as any kind of exercise, but the fact is that a pool session of several hours or more is quite capable of making you good and sore. A player who stays trim, limber, and flexible figures to have a substantial edge.

Now let's take an in-depth look at your shooting stance, in general and one body part at a time.

Your Stance

I can't tell you how to stand for pool. Neither can anyone else.

It may not be the most cheery introduction to this topic that's ever been written, but it's the most honest and most correct. I don't know anything about your dimensions, flexibility, center of gravity, or anything else. Among pool's best players, as we noted about baseball, rarely are any two stances identical. There aren't even as many common denominators among the stances of top players as you might think. It's commonly taught that you should create a straight line between your rear foot, both hands, chin, and cue, and many top players do; but even there, exceptions are not hard to find. We'll examine some of those. For now, remember that the one straight line it's critical to maintain is the one between your shoulder (on the stroking side), elbow, cue, bridge hand, and both balls (cue ball and object ball). It's also wise to remember that *the ultimate objective of your shooting stance is to immobilize every part of your body except your stroking forearm.* (See Photo 1.)

One professional player whose stance has always intrigued me is Florida's Dan DiLiberto, who remarkably has won major titles in each of pool's four major disciplines (straight pool, 8-ball, 9-ball, and one-pocket) in each of four different decades. DiLiberto faces the cue ball almost frontally; the leg on his nonshooting side is practically an innocent bystander to the whole affair. Purists who have never seen him play might be shocked, but DiLiberto is an incredible athlete who has played three sports professionally other than pool (baseball, bowling, and boxing) and could most likely run the table while in a headstand. Might he have been even better had he utilized a more conventional stance? Probably not; that approach is what suits his body best. Without ever having seen him play ball, bowl, or fight, I'd bet sight unseen that at least some of his moves in each were unorthodox.

That's exactly why it's folly for you to attempt to imitate anyone else's stance, no matter how good it looks on that particular player. Even if you have exactly the same size, shape, and flexibility, what guarantee is there that you'd be as comfortable standing that way as your role model is, when comfort has to do with your head as well as your body? It's also why you can't learn stance completely out of a book.

For instance, any number of pro players are approximately my height, a bit over six feet. However, nature presented me with stubby legs that would be proportional to a frame a good three or four inches shorter, but not to mine. Thus my center of gravity is lower than any of those other six-footers (not altogether a bad thing for pool), and it would be absolutely pointless for me to try duplicating any of their stances.

Your Feet

It might seem obvious, but I can't recall any previous pool book pointing this out: as much of a status symbol as it might be to wear certain brands of athletic footwear on a daily basis, you're doing your feet no favors whatsoever to play pool that way (in fact, while your podiatrist might not be eager for you to learn this, your feet would be way better off if you *never* wore athletic shoes except for bona fide athletics). What you're asking your feet to do when you play pool is much closer to everyday functions—walking, stopping, bending—than to athletic endeavors, and heeled shoes will support your feet much better.

A useful adjunct to the above: your choice of footwear is so important here that if you insist on playing pool in different types of shoes—sneakers, loafers, dress shoes, boots, or even shoeless if you play at home on carpet as I do—then you can expect different sets of playing results. You're creating a different foundation for your stance each time, and your muscle memory is going to recognize the differences and quite possibly get confused; and with an altered stance, you're well on your way to grief. Be as consistent in your pool footwear as is practical.

Now, what about where you place your well-shod feet? What's classically taught is, your rear foot and hand should form a straight line with your cue, and that's certainly one way to go. In that sort of stance, your front foot will generally point toward your shot, and your rear foot is angled, though not severely.

Why doesn't everyone stand that way? Because, depending on your frame and build, that may not be the most comfortable way to get your chin over the cue, and that's a must. I've seen good players who made it a point to stand pigeon-toed—not that I recommend such, but it worked for them. Any number of players do seem to favor taking their front foot and hip out of the shot line, although less dramatically than Dan DiLiberto does.

Concerning how wide you should plant your feet, that again is something for you to customize for your own body. But the rule of thumb you should observe is this: Almost every stance in sports is taught with the feet at approximately shoulder width. In pool, it's recommended that your feet be spread slightly past that point. This will help lower your center of gravity and plant you more solidly in your stance. And solidness is just what you want if you're serious about immobilizing everything except one forearm. There are players who function extremely well despite more narrow foot placement than what I've suggested; those players almost invariably compensate for that narrow foot spacing with a more upright stance.

Here's a simple exercise to test the components of your stance. Imagine a surly stranger about to approach you on your shooting side and shove you out of his way. Now imagine being well-planted enough to resist that shove. When you get to the table, you may want to test this with a friendlier source. But if you're that well-set, chances are you've found a stance that will be efficient for you.

Your Knees

I can't think of a single good reason for you to lock your knees in your shooting stance. Any number of players do fall into the unfortunate habit of a straight-legged stance, and such a stance is indeed aesthetically pleasing—but that's not my idea of a good reason. To bend forward without bending the knees is an abomination upon your skeletal frame, and your knees were not designed to withstand much abuse to begin with. You will most likely also be extremely uncomfortable, a sure sign of an ineffective stance. Bending the knees comfortably works in concert with correct foot spacing.

A reasonable exception to this advice that is seen fairly commonly is the stance that plants the back leg as a sort of anchor and bends the front leg; the current number-one ranked and near-dominant woman player, Allison Fisher, stands that way. But she originally learned that stance for snooker, not pool (she was dominant at that, too), and that particular stance is indeed better suited to that particular game, for reasons we needn't explore here.

Your, Well, Rearward Portions

Conventional pool teaching usually overlooks this part of the anatomy, but the fact is that your bottom does have a useful role to play in your stance. It's easy enough (in fact, it's completely natural) to allow that area to droop, having bent your knees—but the buttocks should really be arched in your stance. It will feel a bit peculiar at first, but get into the habit. The advantages are that it's helpful in locking you into the stance, and it pushes more of your weight forward and over the cue, thus more in touch with your shot. The last is of particular value to me because of my pygmy-like pins, and it should help you, too.

Your Torso

Try imagining yourself as an archer; get your lead hand well out in front, and draw back on your imaginary bow. Feel the stretch on your shoulder line? That's how your pool stance should feel, too.

Needless to say, you want no motion from the waist up except for your stroking forearm, and your shoulder on the nonstroking side is going to help you accomplish that. Now is the time for you to find out just how far that shoulder can be comfortably stretched. (With the possible exception of gymnastics, I can't think of another sporting stance or endeavor that tests the same thing.) It's ok to bend your non-stroking elbow slightly, but you still want that shoulder stretched way out there. And leave a little bit in reserve, because pool is going to present you with some really tough or critical pressure shots, and for those you ideally want to be able to stretch even farther.

Over on the stroking side, that elbow should hang more or less naturally, neither jammed into your rib cage nor flapping like a chicken wing. That's a key to your developing a straight swing, as is the disciplining of your stroking wrist to hang straight down without curling either in or out; your knuckles should point right toward the floor at all times. If there is any lateral movement of the cue at all in your stroke, you are most likely not going to advance the cue ball along your line of aim; even if you do, it will be with unplanned sidespin, in which case disaster looms.

Your correct foot placement will help your stroking elbow clear the hip on your backswing without leaving its horizontal plane, a necessity we can't revisit often enough.

Your Forearms

What's commonly taught is that your nonstroking forearm and your cue should form an angle of approximately 45 degrees. I don't disagree with that, but neither would I worry about it if your angle worked out to be 40 or 50 degrees. Your objectives, at any angle, are comfort and stability. If the rest of your body is correctly positioned, your forearm should enter the scene having selected an appropriate angle quite naturally.

As for the forearm that sees to business, there's no overstating its importance; after all, it's supposed to be your only moving body part except for the eyeballs. It should swing straight from the elbow down—in other words, just as it naturally hangs—with no swerving to either side, no matter how the game's pressures torment you. And as long as we've brought in the elbow, let's continue to your upper arm, which ideally is exactly parallel to the floor.

All of this illustrates why it would be such a dandy idea for you to see yourself on videotape. One of the game's finest instructors ever, Jerry Briesath of Madison, Wisconsin, makes that his very first step with every student. Whether your cameraman is a nonplaying buddy or just a fixed-position tripod, there's no better tool for correcting your basics than being able to see your flaws.

Your Head

Your head is simultaneously the area most responsible for your pool prowess and the area most likely to sabotage your shooting stance. No matter how solidly planted you feel, the game's pressures can easily cause you to rear up in midstroke like a frightened stallion, a disastrous "first domino" that usually topples a number of others, including the final destination of the object ball.

As in golf, that other game where you attack an inert white ball on a green surface, head movement is one of the most common and critical flaws of stroke production. Keeping your head in place is largely a matter of confidence plus discipline. Should the flaw persist (and by the way, there are few better substitutes for perfecting your fundamentals than qualified input from a friend, an expert teacher, and/or a video camera), one interesting remedy handed down over the years is this: Stretch an ordinary wire coat hanger into a loop. The loop goes around your neck; the hook attaches to your family jewels. Almost every subject of this experiment has kept his head in place on the very first trial, and all that followed. All kidding aside, however, it would be considerably more practical to accomplish the same thing on your own without physical aids.

Now, exactly where over the cue does your head go in an ideal stance? As classically taught, your cue should be centered directly under your chin. But again, I can't guide you to the very last inch of correctness, this time because of what's called your dominant eye (if you indeed have one; not all do). I can probably guess which of your eyes is dominant—at least 9 times out of 10, it will be the eye on your stroking side—but I have no way of knowing if you'll subconsciously position that eye, instead of your chin, over the cue. A great many players do this, with no negative effects whatsoever. Either way, it's clear that your cue should not be very far removed from the center of your chin.

Just how high over the cue your head should be is yet another area of personal preference, this time with an added bit of advice that runs counter to what you may have already been told. Logic would dictate that you crouch as low as you comfortably can in order to get as close to your work as possible, and I can think of many players who seemed to be carving clefts into their chins. (Most of these same players did begin to stand a bit higher as they aged.) One of the finest cue-games instruction books of all time recommends that your cue brush against your necktie just under the knot (that tip has sociological as well as instructional implications); but once again, that particular advice was offered for snooker, where shotmaking is very, very different from pool.

The last two dominant male pool players we had, Steve Mizerak and Willie Mosconi, who were totally unlike in physical proportions, each assumed a stance in which their heads were about eight inches over the cue. But that information is a two-edged sword, because of the danger of emulating anyone else's stance; additionally, each was dominant in straight pool. The reason that's significant is that successful straight pool depends on your minimizing cue-ball travel. Had those two champions instead played 8-ball or 9-ball, where the cue ball must frequently be moved all over the table, a slightly more upright stance could very well have served them better.

The point of view I prefer, when it comes to head height over the cue, is How low do you *need* to stand? There will definitely be some amount of crouching on your part to ensure accuracy; just as definitely, there is an advantage available to those who can stand a bit higher while maintaining their accuracy, and that is the ability to see the angles of cue-ball deflection, and the paths of its travel, more clearly. This will be a trial-and-error process on your part if you're not working with a teacher, but as a starting point remember that it's not necessary, and may even hold you back, to go just as low as you can.

Your Eyes

As my own vision (if you can call it that) without glasses is 20/400, there isn't much I can do about yours. Try not to get disappointed over this if you wear glasses, but I can't think of a single top-20 player of either gender today who does. Chances are, however, that you do not aspire to join the world's most charmed playing circle, so even if your eyesight needs some correction, you can still become highly accomplished and have a ton of fun.

Where I can help you, however, is with the eyeballs, however keen yours might be. There is an appropriate rhythm to fall into in aiming your shot. When you first settle into your shooting stance, you look at the cue ball, not the object ball, to determine exactly where you want to strike it. (All pool, no matter which form you favor or how complex that game gets, boils down to striking the cue ball accurately, plus bringing your cue forward in a perfectly straight line.) Your eyeballs then alternate from cue ball to object ball, back and forth as many times as you're comfortable with (but do try not to turn your shot into a 20-year mortgage), and the last ball you look at before pulling the trigger is the object ball.

What's far less commonly taught is that there are certain shots where it is definitely to your advantage to look at the cue ball last. These would include shots where the cue ball and object ball are close together, as well as shots where you need to induce maximum cue-ball spin. The latter group of shots is probably responsible for the majority of horrific-sounding and usually fatal miscues; but while you might think that the miscuing player was courting disaster in the first place by straying that far from the center of the cue ball, it's at least equally possible that the miscue occurred because the player was watching the wrong ball.

If you assume more than one stance in your poolplaying, is that a bad thing? Well, yes and no. We've already considered one instance of that, critical shots where I want you to stretch your nonshooting shoulder even farther. Additionally, certain shots, because of tricky reachability, will demand something other than your normal stance. But there are definite limits as to how much stretching for shots you should do. Photo 2 shows my chiseled bodkin in an acceptable stretching stance; note that I still have stroking freedom. That's a key. If I were to stretch so far that my stroke were reduced to a poke or jab, I'd deserve every dreadful consequence imaginable: a miss, poor position, or a miscue (see Photo 3). While it's true that the mechanical bridge is sometimes unchivalrously called "the ladies' aid" and "pimpstick," be assured your virility is not threatened in the slightest way in utilizing it; and you would not believe how many pool games have been lost because a player was simply too lazy to reach for the bridge.

The other aspect of stance consistency for you to consider is this: Every now and then, particularly when you're playing position correctly, the game will reward you with one or more very, very short and therefore seemingly easy shots. It's equally easy to assume a nonchalant stance and execute an indifferent stroke on such shots, and unless the game punishes you for that (as well it should), you're on your way to a cataclysmic habit of failing to bear down on each shot. While there's no pressure on you to sink a ball that's inches from a pocket, you should execute your stance and stroke just the same as if the shot were much longer. It'll pay off.

The other stance well worth learning is the one you take up when you shoot opposite-handed because your desired shot is too hard to reach the conventional way. Why should you bother with that, when the mechanical bridge is readily available for such shots? Because shooting opposite-handed gets you much closer to the cue ball, where your control of the shot is considerably increased. Shots of this nature are likely to be fairly simple ones, once reached correctly, so you needn't fret about playing the entire game equally well with either hand. But you should become proficient enough with your other hand that you can both pocket short shots and initiate appropriate cue-ball action. I learned to do this as a result of playing with my sons; my playing the entire game opposite-handed was their handicap. But beyond that, I had already discovered that adding as little as half a rack of shooting opposite-handed in my practice did wondrous things for my game once I began serious play. The reason for that, at least in my opinion, is that shooting a few balls opposite-handed helps you tap into the side of the brain you don't normally call upon. While time and space do not permit us to get into a full-blown discussion of the psychology of the left and right halves of the brain here, you should know that the very best pool you will ever play will almost certainly be played utilizing your right (nonanalytical, creative) side. Your opposite-handed stance should mirror your regular one; because you're using your unfamiliar shooting hand, most teachers advocate making it a point to take a lighter grip than you would with your favored hand. But be sure your bridge is firm.

Finally, the way in which you take up a proper shooting stance is well worth a look. The correct aiming of a pool shot begins while you are still standing upright; for that reason, you'll be a far more consistent player if you get into your stance the same way each time. Many players execute a jaunty little practice stroke in midair first, theorized to be a technique for recapturing one's inner rhythm. I like to begin by lining up my rear foot and chin with the shot, and then my cue. Next, I set the tip of the cue on the table, approximately where I anticipate putting my bridge hand. (See Photo 4.) At that point, I take a full forward step straight toward the shot (not toward my cue; that's a fairly common error among new players) with my front (left) foot, and pivot on my rear foot so that it forms an angle of 45 to 60 degrees with the front foot. Then I begin to crouch and form my bridge. (See Photos 5, 6, and 7.) But it would be pointless to insist arbitrarily that you do this exactly the same way as I do; just find a routine that lets you do it exactly the same way each time. If, heaven forbid, you ever hit a playing slump, your stance and the way you get into it are among the first elements of your game that you should scrutinize.

We've gone from your feet to your head. Now let's get you a cue.

Your Grip

Before analyzing how you correctly hold a cue, let's consider where you hold it first. (Incidentally, you definitely need your own two-piece cue if you plan to play regularly. While prices for top-of-the-line custom cues today are rapidly approaching psychosis, you can avail yourself of a fine playing instrument for $200 or less, at least for your first cue, in any quality billiards-supply outlet. Do *not* shop for billiard cues where billiards is not the specialty of the house; the lines carried by most retail sporting-goods chains are fair at very best.)

Find the point at which you can lay your cue across two fingers without its tipping either way. That's called, logically enough, the *balance point* of your cue, and you want to grip the cue at least one hand-width in back of that. Six inches behind the balance point is widely considered an ideal gripping location, but taller players with longer wingspans will need a few inches more. You also may wish to take a somewhat longer grip for pool's power shots, such as the break in 8-ball or 9-ball.

Some experimentation will help determine where to grip your cue most comfortably for the way you produce your stroke, but while you're experimenting, remember this (and again, second-party input is invaluable here): you should strive to grip the cue at a point where your stroking forearm will be perpendicular to the table at the moment of cue-ball impact. (See Photo 8.) We'll be getting into the dynamics of stroke production soon, but if your forearm is more than a few inches in front of that perpendicular point at the moment the cue ball is struck, you're going to have a wussy little upward poke at the ball, not a legitimate stroke. (See Photo 9.) If your forearm is aft of that perpendicular point, you will be lifting your cue on your backswing for a choppy stroke, and you'll also be violating one of pool's wisest instructions: keep your cue as level as possible whenever possible. (See Photo 10.) If you're holding the cue too far back, the only way to level it off would be to drop your elbow on your backswing, and no player has accomplished this in the five centuries we've had cue games.

So begin by determining exactly where you want to hold your cue. The next thing to learn is that although all four fingers *cradle* the cue, it's only the forefinger and middle finger that do the *gripping*; your ring finger and pinky are largely along for the ride. (Some highly advanced players even go to a two-finger cradle for *bunts*, meaning very short, easy shots or defensive moves where the cue ball need only be nudged.) The proper instructions for grip tension recall *The Three Bears*: not too tight, not too loose, but just right. Some teach that your palm should be in contact with the cue, but only barely; some insist that there should be no contact; but there's no dispute that a death grip is one of the most common of all beginners' errors. A tight grip will cause a rocking motion in your stroke, hamper your delivery by retarding your wrist action and power, and severely hinder what action you can impart to the cue ball. (Too loose a grip, on the other hand, means a sacrifice in your control of the cue, and accordingly a hindrance in your ability to bring it forward in an absolutely straight line.) A tip many teachers and students find useful: focus on bringing the fingertips of your stroking hand together as lightly as you can. This will practically guarantee that you will not overgrip the cue.

Concerning the thumb, basketball megastar Michael Jordan, said to be a fairly avid pool player, has been photographed with his thumb atop the cue; this is compelling evidence that he should hang onto his day job(s). Your thumb should be wrapped underneath the cue, nowhere else. And, as already stated, *your knuckles point straight at the floor at all times.* No excuse for deviations from the latter will be accepted! Keep your knuckles straight down, and you've gone a long way toward ensuring that your stroking hand is directly under your stroking elbow, right where you want it to be; and that you won't turn your wrist in or out. Both are common beginners' flaws.

The other grip you should learn concerns the ally we just discussed, the mechanical bridge, and your grip on the cue could hardly be simpler: think of holding a pen. (See Photo 11.) (Your nongripping hand holds the bridge steady on the table surface; do not elevate the butt of the bridge unless absolutely, positively necessary because of interfering object balls.) Point the butt of your cue at the center of your chest, no higher. The stroke here is really a quick little jab.

Your Bridge(s)

Let's begin with a maverick point of view: if you follow existing instructions regarding how far from the cue ball your bridge hand should be, you'll be doing yourself a disservice. While almost all references recommend a bridge length of five to eight inches, I firmly believe that shorter is better. For one thing, a shorter bridge obviously means a shorter backswing (otherwise you'd be pulling the cue all the way back through your bridge hand), and a shorter backswing increases your chances of bringing the cue forward in a perfectly straight line, something you know by now that you absolutely must do for an optimal stroke. (See Photos 12 and 15.)

There's an added, more subtle benefit to a shorter bridge. *Feel* is critical to pool playing; that shorter bridge allows you to pull the cue back almost to your bridge hand, which in turn increases your focus on the cue's tip. This will aid you just as focusing on the racket head aids tennis players. Of course, too short a bridge will preclude your hitting the ball with much force at all. But try to stay no more than five inches from the cue ball for most shots; allow yourself a few extra inches for your power shots.

The first bridge you should learn is unquestionably the open-thumb bridge (see Photo 12) that almost every beginner uses (an occasional sub-beginner will utilize what cynics call the "orthodox scorpion bridge," in which the cue wavers haplessly betwixt ring and social fingers; none of that for us). What I'd like you to do a bit differently is learn to take this bridge seriously; it's not just for kids and nonplayers. The open-thumb bridge allows you the most complete view of your playing field, precludes any clenching or tension in the hand, and even increases your reach by a few inches. Besides, it's just about the only bridge used by snooker players, and as noted, they are ungodly shot-makers, firing tiny pellets into teeny pockets on a table so monstrous (6 feet × 12 feet) that it looks like a diorama of an artificial-turf stadium.

In fact, if you never needed to add power to your stroke or spin the cue ball, you'd never need to progress to the loop bridge that all the pros use. Unfortunately, in those situations, it becomes too difficult to control the cue as you'd like. In addition to that, the game's pressures are all too likely to cause your cue to rise like a pheasant off your open thumb, destroying any chance for a level stroke.

Still, for open shots where no special cue-ball speed or dynamics need be introduced, the open-thumb bridge should serve you well—especially, as we noted earlier, if you play less than weekly. It's certainly easy enough to learn. Lay your nonstroking hand flat on the table, fingers together. Now cup it so only the heel of your hand, the base of your thumb, and your fingertips are in contact with the table. Pinch the knuckle of your forefinger with the ball of your thumb, and you're there; the cue rides over the ridge between your thumb and forefinger. (Again, see Photo 12.) Your hand should be cupped enough so your level cue will be pointing at the center of the cue ball. When you want to cue the ball above center, you cup your hand more (what you *don't* want to do is raise the cue instead of your hand). (See Photo 13.) To cue the ball below center, flatten your hand. (See Photo 14.) Your thumb and forefinger remain together no matter what the case; the bases of your bridge—the heel of your hand, the very bottom of your thumb, and your fingertips—stay the same too.

And once that foundation starts feeling familiar and comfortable to you, the transition to your professional (loop) bridge should be an easy one. (Women players, take note: if you maintain long fingernails, those on the thumb and forefinger on your bridge hand, at the very least, should go; the remaining fingernails will do you no particular favors, and may even hinder putting your hand down on the table without disturbing any object balls.) The only real differences are that you now spread the last three fingers instead of keeping them together, and you form a loop between the tips of your thumb and forefinger. That loop then joins your middle finger at the knuckle for added stability. The bases for this bridge are exactly what they were for the open-thumb bridge. Adjust the size of your loop so the cue is correctly guided but neither rubs nor wobbles on the way through; once again, you simply *must* execute your stroke in a straight line in order to play pool at all. As with the open-thumb bridge, you achieve above-center or below-center hits on the cue ball by raising or lowering your hand, not the cue. (See Photo 15.)

Another version of the loop bridge you should learn for limited-space layouts that preclude putting your entire bridge hand on the table: stand your bridge on the tips of your last three fingers, keeping your loop intact. To hit high on the cue ball, arch your wrist. To hit low, lower your hand as best you can, allowing that your reason for employing this bridge in the first place probably means the danger of additional object balls in your way. The nature of this bridge means that your cue will almost certainly be arched to some degree, especially on draw shots, but try not to overdo that. Willie Hoppe, one of the greatest billiards (not pool) players the world has ever known, hit most of his shots with this bridge; but with only three balls on the table, he almost always had room for his bridge so he could keep his cue as level as he wished. That's another game entirely, and you needn't emulate him anyway; but it certainly proves that the bridge, which old-timers used to call the *orthodox tripod*, works. (See Photo 16.)

What if your ring finger sort of "flutters" as you form your loop bridge? It's a good sign, albeit in a subtle way; I'm sorry, but it is not a signal that you are becoming an expert, notwithstanding all the neophytes I've seen giggling in glee at the sight of their first such tremors. Neither is it a precursor to palsy, or any other sort of glum little reminder from life that you have just been welcomed to the downhill side of things. It's just a very simple example of that right-brain activity we discussed in passing; your hand is seeking out firmness and comfort, similar to the way you make minute, subconscious adjustments on the steering wheel even when the road you're driving on is straight and smooth.

One nuance to this bridge that I employ is to create a square instead of a loop by straightening my forefinger from the knuckle down. It changes the opening slightly, which is useful because my hands are not particularly big; at least equally important, it feels more stable and disciplined to me, thus it becomes a factor in my comfort at the table. There's no need for you to make a point of this if it doesn't accomplish the same things for you; it's simply, as *The Twilight Zone's* late genius creator Rod Serling used to say, presented for your consideration.

Getting to the cue ball when it's close to or touching an object ball seems like a sticky task at first, but it's really just a variation on the open-thumb bridge. The distinctions are that your hand now stands on the tips of the last three fingers, and your forefinger is now folded under. The thumb–forefinger ridge is exactly as it was before. The stroke, when you're striking the cue ball above its center, is really more of a flick, to ensure the cue tip gets out of the way without striking the cue ball a second time. To strike the cue ball at or below its center, provided the ball you're bridging over permits you sufficient space to do so, requires a swift downward jab, and naturally you have to get your cue out of the cue ball's path quickly.

No player is happy to see a shot come up in which this bridge must be used, of course, and in correct position play you'll learn to avoid options that might lead you there. But the game is still going to throw such shots at you, no matter how careful you might be, so learn to do this right. By far, the biggest part of learning to shoot over a ball successfully is conquering your discomfort and fear. Strangely and immodestly, I'm more accomplished at this one aspect of stroke production than any number of far better players; and the best single piece of advice I can give you today on shooting over a ball is just what it would have been decades before Nike ever put it into the lexicon: Just Do It. Don't rush such shots, but don't punish yourself by standing over them longer than you have to. And be certain to strike the cue ball exactly in its vertical center; off-center hits with a severely elevated cue will make your cue ball lurch and swerve far from the straight and narrow. (See Photo 17.)

The next boil of Job that pool will visit upon you all too often is the need for various bridges when the cue ball comes to rest on, or very close to, a cushion. (Back in kinder, gentler times, kids used to invoke what was called the "YMCA rule" and permit themselves to move the cue ball one cue-butt's diameter from the rail on such occasions. Today that's a nice way to get yourself lynched.) Your rail shots will come in the form of those in which you're aiming more or less perpendicular to (in other words, away from) the rail; those in which you're aiming more or less parallel to, or along, the rail; and shots in-between. Generally, the first group, while no bargain, is the least troublesome; the second group can be frustrating indeed, as your frustrated fingers scratch and claw for precious purchase. But what's common to all of them is, you first need to provide yourself with an optimal view of the shot—and that means your loop bridge gets a quick vacation, hopefully just one shot's worth. Because your hand is now positioned above the playing surface instead of on it, your raised forefinger in the loop bridge would block your view of the cue ball.

Per Photos 18, 19, and 20, when shooting away from the rail, it's your thumb that doesn't get invited to the party. It folds under, and the cue is guided between your first two fingers. Your equally sensible option to this, especially when the cue ball rests right on the rail, is your familiar open-thumb bridge.

When shooting along the rail on your bridge-hand side, you fold under not only your thumb but the first joint of your forefinger, in effect pinching the cue shaft against the rail. (If your shot were exactly parallel to the rail, or very close to it, you might possibly be able to get away with a version of your regular open-thumb bridge, depending on the size of your hand, where your last three fingers ride the rail. Depending on the cue ball's distance from the rail and the angle of your shot, it's also possible to utilize a version of your loop bridge where your two inside fingers touch the table and your pinky rides the rail.) (Again, see Photos 18, 19, and 20.) Shots along the rail on your *shooting* side are truly a thankless proposition, and should be shunned like The Alien unless you are absolutely out of options. You will even have trouble using the open-thumb bridge here, as your raised thumb is going to force the cue away from the rail. Your best bet is probably a flat palm with the thumb at a point where it's parallel to, but not above, the forefinger, using that mini-ridge for the cue.

The other bridge I want to acquaint you with is downright ungainly. I once had an off-the-wall pool buddy who, when he saw me about to form the *fist bridge* you see in Photo 21, would implore me to put my hand down some other way on the table; he claimed it reminded him of the kids with physical disabilities he used to see begging in Times

Square. Aesthetics aside, the fist bridge is, or should be, wholly functional in your game. As the name implies, you make a modified fist in which all four fingers visit the table surface from the knuckles down, and your first two fingers guide the cue. The fist bridge is to be used only when the cue ball and object ball you're interested in are extremely close together, *and* you need to either stop the cue ball in its tracks or bring it back toward you (*draw* it). (If you were that close to the object ball but wanted the cue ball to follow after it somehow, you'd correctly employ an over-the-ball or some other form of elevated-cue bridge, to help you keep from striking the cue ball twice.) In these situations, the fist bridge allows you the shortest bridge possible, as well as getting you as low on the cue ball as possible while still keeping your cue level; additionally, because you must quickly get your bridge hand out of the way when drawing the cue ball on such shots, the fist bridge affords you a more compact unit to move. Shots in which the fist bridge might be correctly utilized tend to come up more often in pool's finesse games, straight pool and one-pocket, than in 8-ball or 9-ball, and those games are admittedly less popular. But this is a playing tool you definitely should have.

Your Stroke

Now let's set your cue in motion.

If you're serious about not just learning to play pool but improving at it too, it's critical that you make it a point to see good players in action—the better the players, the better for you. The best players, today and always, are found in commercial rooms (with the exception of a small gambling circle of players who only consider very high stakes and remain "underground"). So ask around and determine where there's a "players' room" convenient to you. It's a necessary part of your pool education.

And in following my advice, one thing you're sure to notice is that accomplished players seem to be hitting the ball a variety of ways within the same game. Sometimes there'll be a quick little "pop" of a stroke; other times the stroke will seem longer and more flowing, with the cue tip in contact with the cue ball for a fraction of a second longer. Sometimes the stroke will be executed with the player's wrist locked; at other times, there will be an added wrist flick just before cue-ball contact. The concept of multiple strokes in pool has provoked a debate that shows no sign of abating any time soon. Those arguing against hitting the cue ball more than one way point out that the ball does not know what you've done to it, and anything achieved by a wrist snap can be accomplished just as effectively with a locked wrist; those in support of multiple strokes concede that point, but add that the one-stroke player is working much harder than he has to.

Without taking sides in that ageless feud, I'm convinced that the best advice to those still concerned with their pool fundamentals is to concentrate on one confident, straight, level type of stroke for now. As you become a better player, you may well learn different strokes by feel without their ever being formally taught to you. Even if you do not, that need not necessarily hinder your progress as long as your basic stroke is sound. Consistency goes a long, long way in pool, at all levels.

And on the topic of consistency, one of the most important points to be made in this entire book is this: *You must make a mental commitment to your stroke.* What I mean by that is, certain shots are clearly intimidating to beginning players. You can see it in their body language as they study the shot, and you can certainly see it in their strokes, which are more likely to be jerky, severely abbreviated twitches instead of bona fide strokes. Don't fall into that. Once you've got a shot aimed, no matter how difficult you perceive that shot to be (and, as we'll soon see, it's not even a good idea to form that sort of judgment in the first place), resolve that you are going to strike that shot with the same calm, disciplined, confident stroke you use on your cinch shots. One hand washes the other here; your stroke consistency is one of your greatest allies in eliminating your fear of the balls. Once your stroke is grooved, the mere angles of the balls are little more than incidental.

You already know that the stroke you develop must be both straight and level. What it must also have is a clearly defined, rhythmic beginning, middle, and end, just as any other legitimate athletic strike at a ball. While you'll be adding power and confidence to your stroke as you progress, do not hold yourself back by overhitting the cue ball, an extremely common error among students. One of the reasons pool can be enjoyed by so many different people of all types and ages is that strength is meaningless. In fact, if you were to take your forearm back in your backswing and just let it come forward with gravity without any help from you, that would still be ample force to send the cue ball nearly the length of the table. Try it yourself and see.

As a last pointer before we get into the actual mechanics of stroke production, remember that while you correctly begin aiming a shot before you ever assume your stance, you do nothing whatsoever with your cue *until* you're in your stance. Far too many players are rushing into practice strokes practically before they've begun to bend forward; that only speeds up the entire stroking process, which is bound to end in despair. Some players complete their stance before they even begin to form their bridge; some combine the two; neither nuance is necessarily preferable over the other. But whichever feels more comfortable to you, keep your cue quiet until you're ready for it. That's where stroking rhythm begins.

The first thing you want to do with your cue is to take it into whatever bridge you've chosen and merely point it at the area of the cue ball you wish to hit. Hold it in that position for, say, a second and a half, and integrate your cue mentally into the shot as you've aimed it, both before and after assuming your stance. Then you're ready to begin your practice strokes; let's make you into that rare beginner who actually understands these, what they're supposed to do, and how to produce them for best results.

Practice strokes serve pool players pretty much the way they do baseball players and golfers: *they're a technique for finding your inner rhythm and getting comfortable for the opportunity confronting you.* They are *not* meant to be an approximation of the stroke that is to follow. Can you imagine a batter flailing frantically away with real force before the pitch is even close to being thrown? They'd call the guys with the butterfly nets in short order. Yet you see pool novices seemingly sawing wood with vigor and verve in a useless preshot routine, wasting energy, focus, and time.

Your practice strokes should be at about the same speed as your actual backswing. And that helps explain why so many players overdo their practice strokes; they also rush their backswings, in the hopelessly mistaken belief that their speed backward should approximate their speed forward. It's hard to know why they think that way, but they do; that is simply not true of any move in sports. A pitcher who attempted a windup at the speed of his delivery would fall right off the mound on his duff straightaway; a golfer or tennis player whose backswing imitated the speed of his swing or serve, respectively, would probably whack himself a good one in the head, much as he deserved. Your pool backswing, as with any other sports backswing, should be leisurely and measured. And when in doubt as to its length, remember that shorter makes considerably more sense than longer.

Because of the precise functions of practice strokes as just defined, you want to limit their number. Maybe you've seen a rerun of the marvelous episode of tv's immortal *The Honeymooners* where Ed Norton takes 30 or 40 practice strokes of wildly varying length, pace, and style, while Ralph Cramden fights off apoplexy; hilarious as that may be, there actually are pool dawdlers who play something like that. Three to five practice strokes should be plenty for you, but find a number that feels comfortable and strive to make that number your regular routine, no matter how difficult the shot seems to you. Spending *slightly* more time over the cue ball on especially critical shots is not only permissible but useful; standing there dying because the shot intimidates you, and extending your practice strokes toward the Day of Reckoning so you can put off pulling the trigger as long as humanly possible, is utterly joyless and will almost certainly result in a hapless miss. Trust me, the number and quality of practice strokes are both more important to sound stroke production than you might think.

One more pointer on practice strokes that you should find quite helpful: be sure they take the tip of your cue close to the cue ball. You can't actually touch the cue ball, of course, or you'd be guilty of a foul and would lose your turn; but unless you come close to the ball's edge, your practice strokes are not working as they should to help ensure that you will strike the cue ball exactly where you intend to. As a practical standard, your practice strokes should approach the cue ball closely enough that you can see your cue tip's reflection in the ball's finish. Any number of highly accomplished players have perfected an addressing technique in which they dip the tip of the cue down very close to where the base of the ball actually meets the cloth, but I don't recommend that. There's too much risk of a foul. And besides, you can't hit the ball down there; you might as well aim someplace where you can.

Practice strokes are also an arena for testing your comfort with both your stance and your bridge. In watching tournament play or other meaningful pool competition, you will frequently see players straightening up immediately and abandoning their stance after a practice stroke or two. That either means the player wants to rethink something, or something doesn't feel right, or both. I implore you not to go ahead and set that cue ball in flight until everything feels perfectly right to you, including your aim. The point where I and any number of qualified teachers suggest you check that out is immediately at the conclusion of your last practice stroke. Stop right there, hold everything for a second and a half just as you did when you began your aiming process, and make sure all systems are go. If the shot feels perfect, pull the trigger. If not, straighten up and adjust whatever doesn't feel right. But please do not attempt to adjust aspects of your stance or aim while you're still in that stance; you're odds-on to miss.

Another thing your last practice stroke achieves is to signal the point at which you'll look at the cue ball for the last time and focus on the object ball through your stroke (unless it's one of those types of shots mentioned earlier where it's to your advantage to look at the cue ball last, but those are a small percentage of all shots).

If it's convenient to you, by the way, this would be an ideal time to take this book to a table and apply some of what you're reading (or, if you're serious enough, pick up your cue and practice on the dinner table or desk, visualizing an imaginary cue ball). As I've already stipulated, words only go so far. Pool subtleties like practice strokes and inner rhythm are too abstract to help you if all you do is read about them; they need to be put into practice.

All right, so we've agreed that your last practice stroke and your backswing are going to be a matched set. The length of your backswing will obviously be dictated by the length of your bridge; if it's a hair longer or shorter than it might ideally be (and remember, between the two, shorter is better), we'll happily forgive you for that if you're not rushing and you are taking the cue back in a straight line. A straight backswing will greatly facilitate your ability to bring the cue forward in a straight line as well, and that ability is truly the cornerstone of your pool playing. If your stroke is straight, you're far more likely to contact the cue ball exactly where you plan to; if you do that, your accuracy with the object ball will be greatly enhanced.

Your pristinely straight backswing and delivery do not represent the completion of your stroking responsibilities, however. As in all sports where a ball is struck with something, even the human hand (for example, in volleyball or handball), you are well-advised to *accelerate through the ball*. Perhaps no beginner's flaw is as widespread as tentativeness in the stroke. (The reason for that is that a pool stroke correctly swings from the *elbow*, not the shoulder, and beginners often lack confidence that they can produce enough power with just one forearm. But they can.) While I've already advised you of the folly of overhitting the cue ball, each shot must nevertheless be stroked with authority. And in accelerating through the ball, you're well along to achieving a proper follow-through.

Why does it matter what your cue does after the cue ball is already on its way? Because, again as in all other ball sports, your follow-through is a means, not an end. An appropriate follow-through, besides adding power, permits you to be smooth and fluid throughout your entire swing. Baseball or tennis players or golfers whose swings ended precisely at the point of ball contact would sacrifice just about all their accuracy, power, and efficiency. Because it's not necessary to send the ball very far, relatively speaking, in pool, it's possible to get away with a shorter-than-normal follow-through, and plenty of players do. But it's unnatural, and you might as well begin by learning what comes most naturally.

As a reward for your patience with all the paragraphs thus far, you're finally ready to strike the cue ball. Put it on the head spot where the object balls are racked first; the reason for that will become apparent in a few seconds. Your first assignment is simple enough: aim at the cue ball's exact center, take a comfortable number of practice strokes, pause, and then send the ball into the pocket of your choice at reasonable speed. And, most important of all, freeze.

Exactly where is the end of your cue in relation to that spot where the cue ball formerly sat?

That spot is one of the great teaching aids, not to mention stool pigeons, in the history of the cue games. It will tattle on you every single time if your follow-through is too short. It will also spill its guts without fail if your follow-through is not straight (swerving the cue is another very, very common students' undesirable habit, especially when attempting to introduce some English to the shot). Your cue should be pointing right at the pocket you were aiming at, and nowhere else. If you didn't sink the cue ball, exactly what caused your miss? I'm hard-pressed to think of many possible reasons: you didn't line the shot up correctly, whether through a flaw in stance or aim or both, and/or you didn't deliver the cue in a straight line. (The latter may have occurred because you turned your wrist in or out; both are strictly verboten at all times.) Those aspects need to be analyzed and adjusted as needed. There's nothing to be embarrassed about in not pocketing that cue ball, but the time to catch those possible flaws is right now, at the beginning of things, before your mind and body have any chance to memorize them and turn them into bad habits.

By all means, practice driving the cue ball directly into a hole, and as you improve at it (which shouldn't take long), add speed to your stroke. Practice this until you can feel your confidence in it growing; you should swiftly arrive at a point where you never miss this "shot."

When you reach that point—*and* when the table spot is sending home flawless report cards on your progress—you may then try the same thing using both left- and right-hand English, in either order. (But it'll be awhile before we get to using English on real pool shots.) Again, the spot will be your noble ally, because your stroke for producing English is no different in the slightest way from the one that strikes the cue ball in its center. Your ramrod-straight stroke simply comes through the cue ball at a different point. Any "steering," or cue-swerving, you attempt in producing spin on the cue ball will almost certainly prove detrimental, although it's a terribly easy habit to fall into. Resist it staunchly.

Ideally, you would shun any attempt to play actual pool until you had at least mastered your stroke production to the extent described thus far; that represents the optimal progression for you to be following. Of course, in the real world, you probably want to play and have some fun, which is the true idea of pool in the first place. So let's say this is what you should be practicing on your own, unbeknownst to the opponents you're clowning around with now. Do we ever have some neat surprises for them!

Your Aim

While we'll be getting to object balls and some useful tactics with them shortly in the section on practice, let's talk a bit about where it is you want to send them. I expect you to understand right here and now that the intended destinations for object balls are pockets . . . but I'd be very surprised if you knew the right way to plan that, because I haven't seen it taught often.

If you have played basketball, you probably know the joy of a shot that touches "nothing but net." Even if you don't, you're most likely well-acquainted with the concept of "bull's-eye," or "dead center," or other symbology for perfection. That perception, however, will do you very little good in pool. True, it would be just dandy if you could deliver every single shot to the center of the pocket; since that will not be even remotely possible, let's talk about the most sensible next-best thing.

Stand over any single pocket on a pool table, focus on the pocket jaws, and visually extend the lines they form. If you're standing over a corner pocket, that "funnel" will point at a side pocket; if you're in back of a side pocket, it will point at the opposite side pocket. Resolve right now to accept this bit of aiming discipline: *Only when an object ball lies in one of those imaginary funnels are you permitted to aim it at the center of the pocket.* Any other time, which will represent a substantial majority of all pool shots, you should be trying to *enlarge your target area* by aiming to bounce the object ball in off the pocket jaw farthest from you. And here's why.

Visualize (or actually set up) a shot where an object ball lies very close to a rail. If you look at that shot analytically, I think you'll see that a line drawn from the center of the object ball to the center of the pocket will intersect the rail about two-thirds of the way down—just as your object ball is likely to do, if you insist on aiming it that way. But a line drawn between that object ball and the pocket jaw visible to you touches nothing, and shots sent along that line will go cleanly home. Learning to carom in your shots this way will vastly improve your game virtually at once. Even tables that cater to serious players by having sinister things done to them to narrow the pocket mouth—the so-called "tough pockets"—yield to this technique. See Diagrams 1 and 2.

Now that you understand what you're correctly aiming at, let's consider what you aim. If you've ever seen pool played at all, you've probably seen a player point his cue at the object ball in the direction of a pocket, as a prelude to aiming. There's nothing wrong with that particular aid—but technically speaking, it's not quite aiming, either. It only gives you a starting point. The player pointing at an object ball that way is trying to visualize the cue ball in contact with the object ball precisely at the point he's sighting. But the catch is, that technique will only work when the shot points straight to a pocket to begin with (or, in pool jargon, is *straight-in*); and in that case, the player wouldn't bother pointing through the object ball anyway.

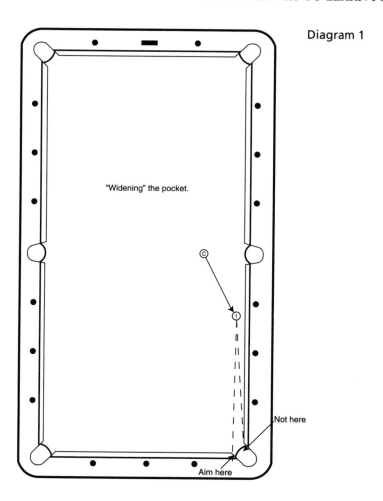

Diagram 1

"Widening" the pocket.

Not here

Aim here

What we're talking about here is the phenomenon pool calls *cling*. The term refers to friction between cue ball and object ball. When spheres of identical size and weight collide, friction causes them to cling together for a tiny fraction of a second before deflecting off one another. This effect can be minimized only by a set of perfectly clean, well-polished balls, and those can be very hard to find indeed; even then, the cling effect must be compensated for to some degree, and it gets considerably more pronounced as the balls become dirty (not real "dirt" as much as accumulated moisture in the air, grease from players' hands, and dust from the air and cloth).

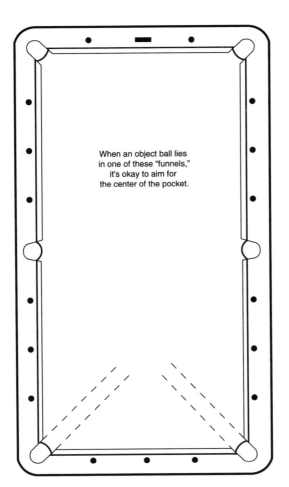

Diagram 2

When an object ball lies
in one of these "funnels,"
it's okay to aim for
the center of the pocket.

Because of cling, any shots other than straight-ins should be aimed *slightly past* the point of aim you'd normally find by pointing your cue at the object ball. Words fail me in emphasizing just how important this is. As an example, the lion's share of pool instructional books that deal with this subject teach that to sink an object ball touching ("frozen to," in pool lingo) a cushion, the cue ball should contact the object ball and the rail at the same time. But those books have not considered cling, and their advice will have you producing misses that make you mutter, "Not even close!" Because of the cling effect, a cue ball contacting an object ball that way is going to "throw" that object ball toward the rail before sending it on its way. On rail shots, your cue ball should contact the rail slightly in front of the object ball, perhaps as much in front as the width of a credit card.

You can easily prove this yourself. Place two object balls along the rail, touching both the rail and each other. Have a buddy stand over those balls. You and he count to three, whereupon he pulls the object ball closest to you out of the way and you try to replace it with the cue ball. I'll bet my mortgage you do not sink the remaining ball—in fact, you'll miss it by a mile—and the culprit will have been cling.

Despite all these caveats, aiming is undoubtedly the easiest of all pool basics. You should become as adept at aiming as the world's great players are in the space of just a few hours. (A considerable gap between you and them will still exist, however, but we're working on that.) It's not hard to see what needs to be done. The trick is in doing it.

With that in mind, you should see that aiming *combination shots*, in which you use one object ball to pocket another, is not wildly different from aiming conventional ones. You merely aim the first object ball at the second just as you aim your cue ball at the first, and you must allow for cling in both ball-to-ball contacts. That's another pretty fair reason to avoid combination shots, early in your development, that don't form a line fairly close to a pocket just as they lie.

Cueing the Ball

Obviously, the biggest, fattest part of the cue ball for you to hit is its exact middle, and that's as good a reason as any that beginners are often taught shotmaking just that way. It's also the point of contact at which cue-ball control is simplest. Unfortunately, the game is going to demand that you cue the ball elsewhere from shot to shot, if you expect decent position for your next shot each time. So the least you're going to have to learn is to get comfortable with striking the cue ball up and down its vertical center.

In fact, one theory of pool instruction is that you need to learn very little else, because sidespin (that is, left- or right-hand English) is only to be resorted to in extreme situations. Back when straight pool was still king, its best players in the world were all but unanimously from the East Coast; almost as unanimously, they stayed in the vertical center of the cue ball. However, the game of straight pool is all about minimizing cue-ball travel from shot to shot. The games that are played most commonly today, 8-ball and 9-ball, frequently require you to travel all over the table as you avoid obstacles in the form of interfering object balls, and that means you should ultimately learn to use the cue ball's equator, too.

But let's define some practical limits first. Whenever table layouts call for you to cue the ball either above or to either side of its center, do *not* stray farther from that center than halfway to the ball's edge (in other words, the outer quarter of the ball is off-limits). When you risk cueing the ball closer to its edge than that, you gain very little incremental spin and put yourself in grave danger of a miscue.

That same rule, however, does not apply when you want to bring the cue ball back toward you, or draw it. This is one of the more difficult basics for beginners to master, and a primary reason for their trouble is their lack of confidence in cueing low on the ball. On those shots, you should cue the ball as low as feasible, as in Diagram 3 (keeping your cue level, of course). Striking the cue ball a cue-tip's width or so below center simply does not create sufficient backspin to create the effect you want. (There are shots where that type of execution is required, though; we'll get to that.)

With that foundation in mind, what can be done with a cue ball? Let us count the ways.

• **Dead-center hit.** Assuming your cue is level at the point of contact, this hit will make the cue ball skid at first, before taking on a natural roll. How far it skids before beginning to roll is a direct function of how hard you hit it. If it's still skidding when it meets an object ball, and it meets that ball full in the face, as it would on a straight-in shot, it will stop in its tracks (but, and this is important, it will not take the place of the object ball it struck; it will stop exactly one ball's width away). If, however, it deflects to either side of the object ball after skid-

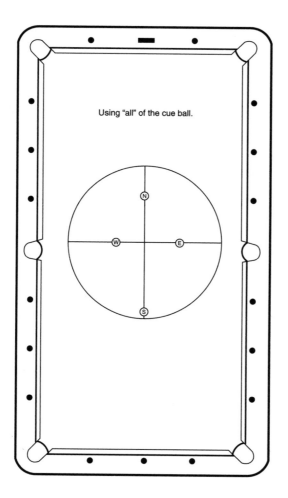

Diagram 3

Using "all" of the cue ball.

ding into contact, *it will deflect 90 degrees from the object ball's path*. This is known as the *90-degree rule* or *rule of tangents*; by either name, this and its corollaries (which follow) are a cornerstone of position play. Learn it now and well. Please.

• **Just-above-center hit.** Actually, this type of hit, no more than a cue-tip's width above center and often less, has very limited application. You use it when you're forced to play position in tight quarters, and you want no more than a ball's width or so of cue-ball travel after contact, but you don't want to stop it dead. Then a soft stroke and a just-above-center hit will get the job done.

• **Above-center hit.** When you want the cue ball to follow after the object ball it's struck, and for a good percentage of your angled shots too, you need to get comfortable with striking the cue ball three quarters of the way up its vertical middle. This creates the natural roll you'd expect, and a ball rolling this way will deflect *less than 90 degrees from the object ball's path* on all angled shots.

• **Left- or right-hand English.** This is an aspect of play that leads far too many beginners astray. The correct times to use English, at least while you're still learning the game, are when there are good reasons to. You must not select it arbitrarily because you think you need to or you just enjoy seeing the ball spin. Good reasons include altering the cue ball's path to avoid an interfering object ball or scratch, or changing its angle of rebound off a cushion. Still, just as the straight-pool era spawned a school of thought that said the game could be mastered in the cue ball's vertical center, there's an opposing species of players who favor working with every last hittable smidgen of the cue ball. They're called *tip players*, and they hit almost all their shots, regardless of length or angle, at just about the same speed, achieving the desired cue-ball dynamics and travel through spin. (The center-ball players are called *speed players*, because in lieu of spin, they must measure how hard to hit each shot.)

Once again, I can't think of a single reason for you to cue the ball any farther from its center than that three-quarters-of-the-ball limit we talked about, and on many shots, unlike your follow shots, less far than that will still get the job done. What beginners frequently find difficult about spinning the cue ball is the ability to deliver a straight stroke through anyplace but the cue ball's center, and that soon leads to the deadly habit of "steering" the stroke. We'll have none of that, please. Stroke straight through the ball no matter where you cue it.

Center sidespin does not affect angles of cue-ball deflection off the object ball.

• **Just-below-center hit.** Closely related to the just-above-center hits; you strike the cue ball here when you again want minimal travel after object-ball contact. The difference is that you use this instead of just-above hits when the cue ball and object ball are farther apart and you need to hit the cue ball harder.

• **Draw-shot hit.** If you expect to bring the cue ball back toward you with consistency, you simply must develop your confidence to cue the ball a good two cue-tips' width below its middle. Keep your cue level and your rear hand relaxed—two things beginners fail to do all too often—and stroke with confidence. It seems tricky at first, but stay with this. You've got to have it. The ball must be backspinning toward you at the moment of object-ball contact in order to create the draw effect. When you use draw on angled shots, instead of coming back toward you the cue ball will deflect at an angle *in excess of 90 degrees* from the object-ball path.

• **English in combination with follow or draw.** Since this area clearly represents the most sophisticated aspects of cue-ball control, you should be certain that your shot really requires all this before you embark. The reasons you'd resort to this dual technique are as stated in the previous discussion of English (page 35), *plus* your desire to alter the angle of deflection off the object ball to something other than 90 degrees.

As stated, an above-center hit on the cue ball will cause a deflection angle of less than 90 degrees; a below-center hit, assuming the cue ball is still backspinning at object-ball contact, will produce an angle of deflection greater than 90 degrees (how much more or less is a function of cue-ball speed). Things get a bit muddled when factoring sidespin into deflection angles, though. As stated, center sidespin doesn't affect deflection; but in my experience, so-called "inside English"—that is, English on the same side of the cue ball as the direction of the cut shot—used in combination with draw widens the deflection angle considerably. We'll take a closer look at inside English later on; as far as position play goes, it's one of the game's great secrets.

Shotmaking

While shotmaking is not all there is to pool, nor even remotely close, you're obviously not going far in the game without it. After all, if you were a good enough shotmaker, at least in theory it wouldn't make much difference where you left the cue ball each time; and many intermediate-and-better players whose position play is flawed are able to bail themselves out with their pure shotmaking ability. It'd be wonderful if you had that kind of ability. But since few do, and it's not the proper way to play the game anyway, let's not make you dependent on that.

I firmly believe that there's an advantage to regarding pool shots a bit differently from the way you do now. I'm talking about most beginners' tendency to classify shots as "easy" or "hard," with many novices putting heavy emphases on the latter. Be a bit analytical about it, and you'll see that the shots most often referred to as "hard" are really those in which the shooter has a less frontal view of the correct point of aim. And that's all. When you have to make the cue ball strike an object ball way out on its edge (or, as it's called, "cut it thin"), isn't that the real problem? That you have to imagine the point of contact, as opposed to seeing it clearly?

Why is that harder? The point of aim is still available to be struck. Your confidence in doing that may waver because you don't like the view, but the shot remains perfectly makable. What makes it hard is simply the negativity you're bringing to it. So why not abandon all that baggage, and simply start thinking of pool shots as just shots, without any judgments as to how hard they are? Sure, it's easier to talk about than do, but it will pay off virtually at once. You'll spare yourself oodles of pressure, your attitude toward the game will be vastly improved, and your playing progress will leave your buddies in the dust.

Here's an easy way to prove that such misperceptions exist. Put the cue ball in the exact middle of the table, and set an object ball about six inches from a corner pocket, creating an angled or "cut shot." Shoot it in, noting your confidence level with the shot. Now set another object ball up in the same line as the first but 12 inches farther away from the pocket, and move your cue ball over to compensate so you now have the exact same angle as your first shot, only it's longer this time. (Diagrams 4 and 5.) Shoot it in. How confident did you feel that time, and how did you do? If your confidence is unshaken, great; you're on your way. If you got a bolt from the blue flashing "harder" as you contemplated your shot, ask yourself why. It was, for all intents and purposes, the identical shot. You had the same point of aim; all you had to do each time was deliver the cue ball in a straight line to that point of aim. So what was harder about it?

Another species of shot that beginners are often unhappy to see is the cutting of an object ball that rests on, or very close to, a rail. And an excellent way to overcome that particular fear is to set the shot up at the angle you dislike but with the object ball reasonably close to the pocket. (See Diagrams 6 and 7.) When you can make the shot at that distance 8 times out of 10—a ratio several teachers consider key—move the object ball farther up the rail (say one diamond's worth), replicate the angle, and test yourself again. This self-improvement process should work for any given shot that intimidates you, if you have the patience to apply it.

Therefore, we can agree your comfort level with pool shots in general increases as the object ball gets closer to either the cue ball or the pocket. Even when you have to drive the object ball some distance, don't you like it better when you don't have to send the cue ball far to start it on its way? Even when the object ball is some distance from the cue ball, don't you like it better when you don't have to drive it far into the hole?

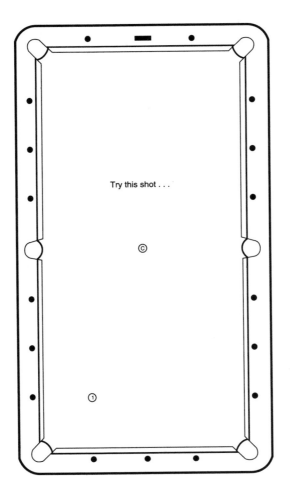

Diagram 4

Try this shot . . .

That's precisely why shotmaking is often taught utilizing shots in which the object ball lies precisely halfway between cue ball and pocket; such shots take away any psychological edge the student might have and force him to meet the challenge properly. You measure these intervals, again, by the diamonds on the table rails (they are far more functional than being merely decorative).

Let's accept that premise and consider an ideal application for you as you get comfortable with pool shotmaking (and if the term *comfort*

Diagram 5

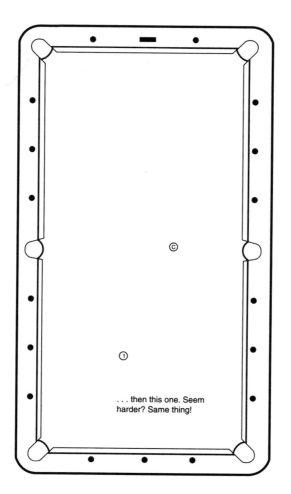

. . . then this one. Seem harder? Same thing!

and its derivatives seem to be popping up to the point of overuse, that is intentional; pool is played as much in your head as on a table). Warming up with short shots should not embarrass you in the least; it's anolagous to the golfer who warms up on the putting green, starting from just a few inches away instead of on the driving range. That's what smart golfers do.

So string 10 balls across the table, one diamond away from the corner pocket, and place your cue ball at the second diamond, as in Diagram 8. For each shot, place the cue ball exactly in line with your intended ball and pocket (the reason we begin with straight shots rather

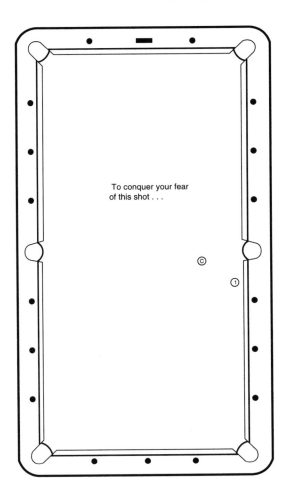

Diagram 6

To conquer your fear
of this shot . . .

than angled ones is because straight shots spare you having to compensate for any cling). Strike the cue ball in its exact center, try to hit it with enough speed that it stops dead on object-ball contact, and see if you can pocket 8 out of those 10 balls, placing the cue ball manually each time.

This drill has an added nuance: be sure to observe *exactly* what your cue ball does upon contact with the object ball. Assuming you line each shot up correctly, a straight stroke delivery and accurate center-ball hit should stop the ball dead in its tracks—no spin, no roll, nothing. If there's any cue-ball motion after striking the object ball, no

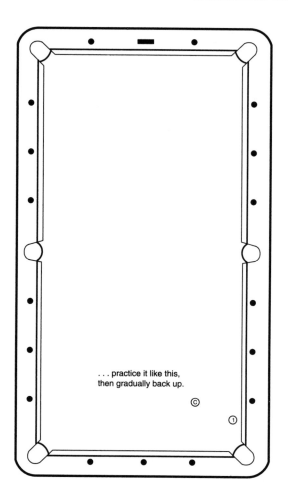

Diagram 7

. . . practice it like this,
then gradually back up.

matter how seemingly insignificant, it means that you're not exactly in the center of the cue ball, or you're not keeping your cue perfectly level, or possibly both. And that will help serve as a reminder that hitting the cue ball precisely where you intend to is not quite as easy as it might seem.

When you can hit the 8-of-10 mark from there consistently, promote yourself to a 3-to-1½ ratio (that is, your object-ball string 1½ diamonds from the pocket, your cue ball along the third-diamond line). When that benchmark falls to your mastery, continue to 4-to-2, and so

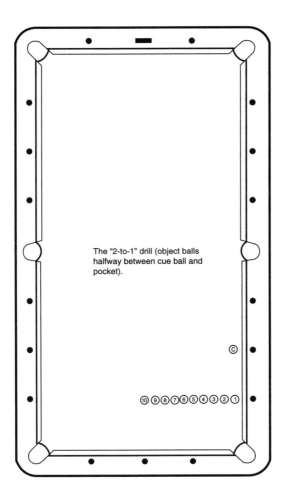

Diagram 8

The "2-to-1" drill (object balls halfway between cue ball and pocket).

on. (Don't concern yourself with taking this exercise to the ultimate of 8-to-4, at least not for now; that's professional level.) Continue as long as you can pocket 8 of the 10 balls consistently.

Your logical next step would be to introduce some versatility to the drill. Instead of taking on that line of balls as straight-in stop shots, practice them using above-center (follow) hits on the cue ball, then below-center (draw) hits. Strive for a given amount of cue-ball travel, say, all the way to the end rail on your follow shots, and back to where you began on the draw shots. Then adjust your cue-ball placement so

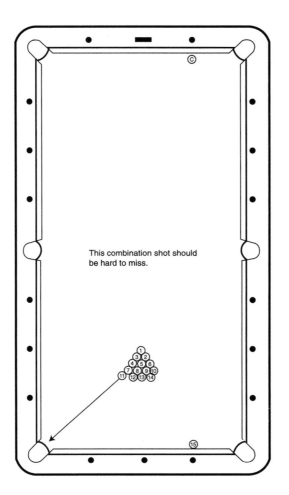

Diagram 9

This combination shot should
be hard to miss.

that instead of shooting the balls straight in, you have to hit them at an angle or cut them. And finally, practice the drill using sidespin on both sides.

Why don't I suggest that you practice shotmaking simply by rolling balls out on a table, so you're confronted with shots of varying angle and length? Because that isn't *structured*; and as with many disciplines, structured practice will work far better to develop your skills than free-form exposure. However, since we've already stipulated that the principal purpose here is to have fun, I don't propose to turn your

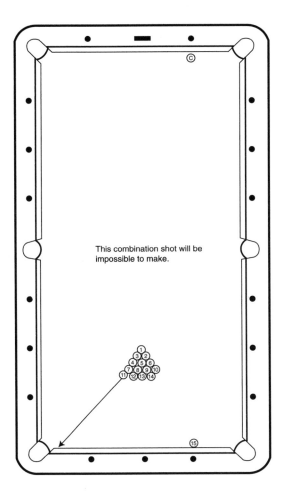

Diagram 10

This combination shot will be impossible to make.

practice sessions into outright drudgery. Shooting balls off a table at pure random does have its place. But I'm quite certain that you'll have a lot more success at it, and thus enjoy it far more, if you'll reward yourself with it after some drills first. The reason is that the drills require you to repeat the same body moves time and again, because of the similarity of the successive shots, and so your basics get "grooved." By the time you're ready to take on balls scattered at random, your muscle memory will have kicked in, and you should feel quite a bit more confident about all kinds of shots.

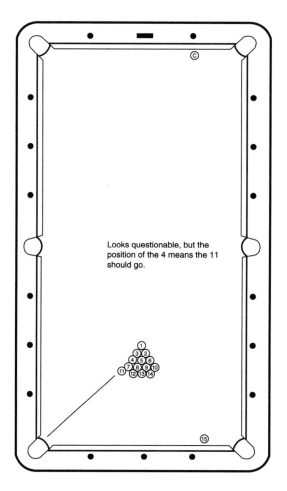

Diagram 11

Looks questionable, but the
position of the 4 means the 11
should go.

The Other Shots

What about those layouts where you can't simply drive the first object
ball you hit cleanly into a hole?

That doesn't mean you can't still score. Even before we get into
defensive play, there may be offensive options available to you in the
form of *combination shots* (either readily apparent ones or "hidden"
ones out of a clustered group of balls); *caroms* (in which you send the
first object ball into another and then to a pocket); *billiards* (in which
the cue ball deflects off a first object ball into a second, and sinks the

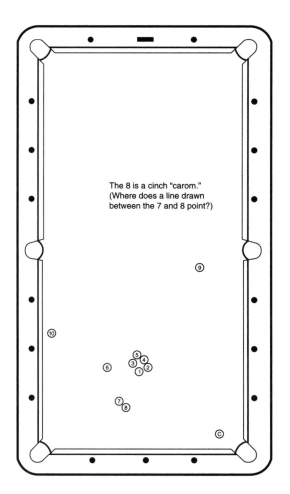

Diagram 12

The 8 is a cinch "carom." (Where does a line drawn between the 7 and 8 point?)

latter); and *bank shots* (in which you bounce the object ball off at least one cushion before it finds a hole).

We can't diagram them all, of course, but we can consider the basic premises of each.

We've already considered basic combination shots, in which you aim one object ball into another. Discovering hidden shots in a cluster of balls is a real art, and even in pool's advanced ranks, some players are much better at this than others. Your first lesson here is simply to remember to look for them, both when you first come to the table after your opponent's turn has finished and when you alter a cluster, or

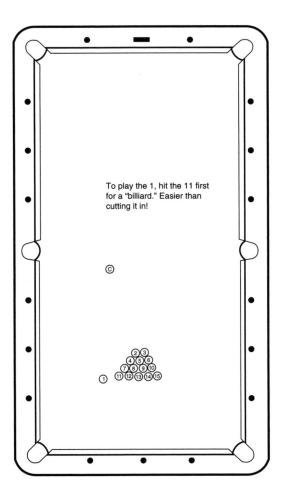

Diagram 13

create a new one, yourself. The favorable signs you're looking for in a cluster are as follows.

• Two balls whose line points at a pocket. If you can hit the second ball—not the one you intend to pocket—with the cue ball directly, fire away. If, however, there are more than two balls in the line, the third ball (that is, the one twice removed from your intended object ball) is the one you use to gauge the potential of your shot. If that third ball does not lie in the same line as the first two, then it's going to alter that line, perhaps by as much as one inch for every foot of length to the shot

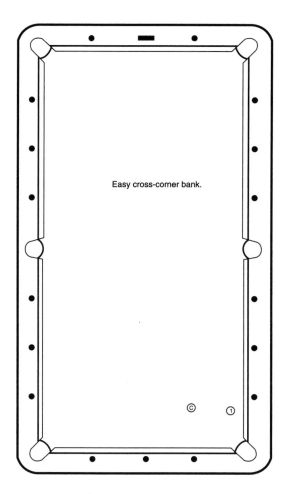

Easy cross-corner bank.

Diagram 14

(less than that if you hit the shot hard, but it's definitely going to realign the shot in some way). Conversely, if the line of the first two balls points close to, but not directly at, a pocket, the third ball may be positioned so as to make the difference you need. Remember that this "throwing-off" effect is maximized at lower cue-ball speeds, and it only exists when the object balls in question are within one-quarter inch of one another or less. If, for instance, your object-ball tandem points slightly to the right of a pocket, and the third ball removed is going to approach that tandem from the right, you're in business; the desired object ball will be thrown to the left. (Diagrams 9 and 11.) If the third

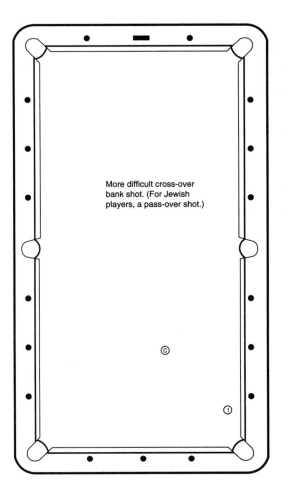

Diagram 15

More difficult cross-over bank shot. (For Jewish players, a pass-over shot.)

ball approaches your tandem from the left, however, the shot can only lead to tears. (Diagram 10.)

• Two balls that lie side-by-side so that a line drawn between and perpendicular to them points at a pocket. Such shots can be made to work whether you hit your intended object ball directly or drive another one into it; in the former case you have a carom, and in the latter a combination/carom. Again, you want no more than one-quarter inch between the two object balls. Diagram 12 shows you a typical carom.

• Somewhat related to the aforementioned is the situation where two object balls are spaced one ball's width or less apart, but a line drawn between their edges still points to a pocket. While a carom here would be highly risky at best, a billiard could very well get the job done, as in Diagram 13. And, as you might expect, the game will also present you with hybrids; for example, a combination/carom/billiard, in which you send a first object ball off a second and into a third, and the latter is the ball to be pocketed. Such shots may be complex to read about, but they'll become much more clear and simple once you've had some experience at the table. Billiards come up less frequently than either combinations or caroms, and are harder both to find and make—because unlike those first two categories, they can be affected by where you strike the cue ball and its resultant deflection off the first object ball.

• Bank shots, in which your intended object ball must visit a cushion before a hole, can first be introduced according to the "bisect the angle" principle you learned in high school geometry. Unfortunately, in pool, that premise only goes so far (although you've got to begin someplace). You'd expect a pool ball to come away from a cushion at the same angle at which it arrived, but that's not nearly as infallible as you might think. While theoretically true, the theory goes awry in practice any time balls are struck hard; if an object ball is skidding (as a common result of being really whacked) when it contacts a rail, the angle going out will be much more shallow (*shorter* in pool parlance) than the angle going in; ditto if the table cloth is new, which tends to make balls skid more than they naturally would. Less-than-perfect cushion rubber, table cloth, and levelness can also be factors in unpredictable bank-shot rolls.

Pool bank shots are truly a complex matter, but the right way for you to approach them as a beginner is to learn the angles of deflection off a rail using the cue ball alone. Place it in front of a side pocket, for example, and aim it directly at the second rail diamond away from you; at moderate speed, the cue ball should bounce into a corner pocket. But turn up its speed, and you won't get the same results. Now extend your practice so your objective is to bank the cue ball into a pocket from anyplace on the table you select. You'll soon develop a feel for what might work and what has no chance. Your actual bank shooting won't be anywhere near that easy—after all, you must be accurate enough to deliver the object ball to the correct spot on the rail—but at least you'll have an appropriate foundation. (You'll also learn that an object ball's angle off a rail can be affected by both cue-ball direction and spin, making some seemingly impossible bank shots quite feasible.)

Speaking of that, you should also recognize that bank shots fall into two categories: those in which you simply drive the object ball ahead into a rail, and those in which you shoot the cue ball past, or across the face of, the ball you're trying to bank (Diagrams 14 and 15). Shots in the latter category will not result in the same angle of deflection off the rail for the object ball as it would take in the first category. The reason is that a cue ball approaching and crossing an object ball from the right, say, will impart left-hand English to the object ball, and vice versa, no matter what spin the cue ball was struck with; thus the object ball will come off the rail at a slightly wider angle than it normally would. These shots may sound exotic, but they come up all the time in 8-ball and 9-ball, so you need to be ready for them.

Photo 1
My stance from the front.
Note stretch of lead shoulder
and head–cue relationship.

Photo 2
Acceptable stretch. I still control the
cue.

Photo 3
Unacceptable stretch. I don't control
the cue.

Photo 4
Step 1 for getting into stance: Face
shot frontally and point
cue at shot.

Photo 5
Step forward with front foot.

Photo 6
Pivot rear foot about 45 degrees.

Photo 7
Begin to crouch and form bridge.

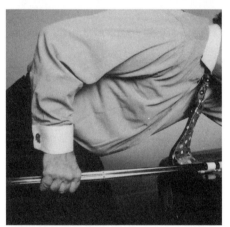

Photo 8
Stroking wrist in correct
(perpendicular) position at moment
of contact.

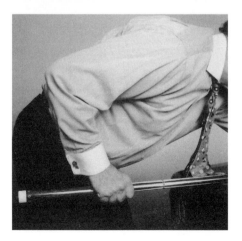

Photo 9
Stroking wrist too far forward at
moment of contact.

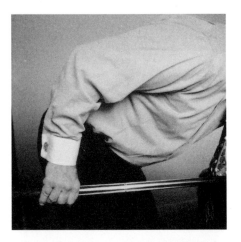

Photo 10
Stroking wrist too far back.

Photo 11
Correct grip(s) for mechanical bridge.

Photo 12
Open-thumb bridge.

Photo 13
Open-thumb bridge raised. Note that I raise my hand, not the cue.

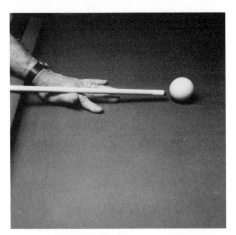

Photo 14
Open-thumb bridge lowered. Again, just lower the hand.

Photo 15
The loop bridge. I point the forefinger, but you don't have to if it feels unnatural.

Photo 16
Loop bridge, raised or tripod version.

Photo 17
Bridging over a ball.

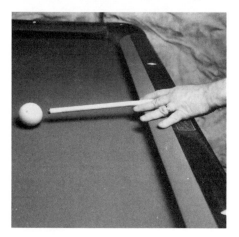

Photo 18
Rail bridge.

Photo 19
Rail bridge for another angle, bridge-hand side of table.

Photo 20
Rail bridge for another angle, shooting-hand side of table.

Photo 21
Fist bridge. Homely, but effective when cue ball and object ball are close together.

PLAYING THE GAME—PHYSICALLY AND MENTALLY

Suppose I taught you the rules and general format of poker for the first time, which should take no more than 20 to 30 minutes. Would you then immediately seat yourself at the nearest high-stakes game? (If so, I know of several that will pay your cab fare both ways.)

This again illustrates the danger of learning things correctly by rote in the absence of practical application. Your foundation of sound pool basics is absolutely essential to your becoming any kind of player; after all, there isn't much to the physical side of pool besides those very same basics. On the other hand, your knowledge of pool fundamentals in and of itself, even if you can pocket a few balls reliably, will still leave you all but helpless in playing the game.

And those last three words are a key as to why more pool beginners don't progress to intermediate stages and beyond. The vast majority of good pool players are good *game* players too, skilled at backgammon, chess, or cards, and sometimes all of them. Although the lion's share of recreational pool is played by beginners as a matter of knocking balls into holes, there's so much more to the game than that. It's true that you could beat a lot of people merely by becoming a very good shotmaker. But you'd still be a fair, and very juicy, target for opponents who take a more advanced approach to playing the game. Better 8-ball players would bedevil you with table layouts that are terrific for them but terrible for you, just as a chess player would. Better

9-ball players would think farther ahead than you, just as a good card or backgammon player would.

I have little doubt that this topic is worth a book or maybe volumes on its own. But for now, understand that you will improve markedly once you begin *to perceive pool as a matter of stopping the cue ball someplace favorable.* Almost everybody else will be focused on putting balls in holes; you be smarter than that. Learn to take it for granted that the object ball will be in the hole if you aim and execute your stroke properly, and dwell instead on the travels of your cue ball. That's how the game is really played. Pocketing a single ball is all but meaningless (unless that lone ball is all you need to win); the whole idea is to figure out how to send—and stop—your cue ball someplace favorable to another shot while pocketing a ball. Shotmaking is a *requirement* if you expect a second consecutive turn, but you simply must get past the notion that it's the end-all and be-all of the game.

I'm not merely admonishing you that you must play position while sinking your shots (although that's certainly part of it). The idea is to get you to start looking at pool as a matter of creative problem solving: How can I move the cue ball from where it is now to point (or area) X, allowing that I have to put an object ball in a pocket at the same time? A top hustler once told me something that I found very wise: "You and I can watch the same pool game for hours, and you still won't see the same game I do." This is the game I want you to see: from the point of view of the cue ball. Let its white purity be your guide; this is where your concentration should be invested.

Try this simple experiment: set up a shot of your choice that you can make, nothing too easy, and shoot it right now, before you read another word.

Now that you've done that, let me ask you this: did you follow the object ball on its way to the hole?

Why?

Obviously you can't do anything about its flight, once it's on its way. So you might as well *follow the cue ball visually* instead. You can't do anything about its travels, either, but getting into this habit—significantly trickier to achieve than it is to read about—will vastly improve both your focus and your technique for moving the cue ball around the table. You'll also find it easier to keep your head down during stroke production when you don't look up to sneak a peek at where the object ball is headed. If you're shooting a straight shot and you want the cue ball to stop dead, focus on that stopping: how it sounds, how it looks, and most of all, how it *feels*. If you execute your cue-ball kill correctly, the object ball will automatically be in the hole. Stop shots are the easiest in which to apply this new technique, since there's zero cue-ball travel involved after contact with the object ball, but with practice you can bring this new focus to every shot on the table.

This method of focus, which may well alone be worth the price of this book, is part physical and part psychological—and for the physical part, the only adjustment you have to make is with your eyeballs. However, if you are serious at all about maximizing your improvement at pool, there's another adjustment that will be necessary, this time with what's behind your eyeballs.

Pool is subject to all the same distractions golf is; after all, there is no real opponent except the game itself, and you're attacking an inert white ball on a green surface in both endeavors. Actually, pool is considerably closer to putting than to golf, given the space constraints, and what veteran putters call *the yips* are all too available to pool players. I don't play golf myself, but I know many who do—and besides, I've done considerable reading on it because of the similarities to pool that I perceive, and I'm quite certain that the yips correspond to the inner voices we hear all the time. In pool, the voices usually state all the possible negatives in a situation: *You miss most shots like this. You overcut them to the right, as a matter of fact. If you miss this shot that way, or any other way, your chances of losing will be greatly increased. The twelve people watching this game will think you're a loser and a dog. The guy you're playing is really just taking advantage of you, and you can't win,* and on and on. Since this clearly won't do, and we've been taught since childhood that it's quite impossible to make your mind completely blank, what are we going to do about those voices?

I can't explore the inside of your head, but in my experience a great deal of that goes away when you stop focusing on the object balls. The first way I was ever able to accomplish that was to sensitize myself to the feel of my cue against the cue ball. Differently constructed cues can definitely be told apart; generally, metal-jointed cues tend to feel more absorbent or mellow upon contact with the cue ball, and ivory- or synthetic-jointed cues feel more stiff. Whatever your preference turns out to be, by all means get in touch with that feeling. It's a good place for your focus; further, it will get you started playing by feel instead of reason, a dandy thing to happen. Once you get good at this, try to develop your feel for the cue ball's spin (if any), and for cue-ball–object-ball contact, too. You might wonder how you can feel a collision between two spheres unconnected to your body, but you can; a stop shot where you hit the object ball full in the face truly feels different in your gut than a thin cut shot does, and with experience you'll learn to perceive the difference.

What I added next was the follow-the-cue-ball technique described previously. So between that and the ethic of "feel the ball," I had pretty well pushed the object ball out of my thoughts, once I had the shot aimed. And that resulted in a new degree of mental calm and improved focus. But recently—and I can't begin to explain why this took over 40 years to come across—I fell into the habit of simply dwelling on my stroking hand and the straight line it was inscribing. Now I had eliminated cue, cue ball, *and* object ball from my perspective—and while I can't guarantee this will work equally efficiently for you, I enjoyed an improvement of about 15 percent within just a few days.

Okay, let's say your stroke production is coming along as you'd like, both physically and mentally. How are you going to apply that foundation to pool's most popular forms?

You begin by looking at those games a bit differently from the way you do now. Straight pool, for instance, is the only pool game that theoretically permits you to shoot any ball into any pocket at any point during the game. Does that mean it's the easiest game? No, actually it's one of the hardest, because of all the options confronting you. Far more than the other two games, straight pool will present layouts that include both object balls available for open shots and clustered balls that must be moved somehow. Thus the game becomes a matter of learning which balls to leave alone (and how you go about that), and which to attack.

Eight-ball, correctly seen, becomes a matter of deciding when to pocket balls and when not to. Yes, you read that sentence correctly; 8-ball, far more often than you think, dictates situations in which *the correct game-playing move* involves making no shots. This is not an easy mental adjustment to make; after all, knocking balls into holes would appear to be pool's primary objective. (But you're already smarter than that, right?) Anybody who perceives 8-ball as a race to see who can clear their striped or solid balls plus the 8 off the table before the other player does is begging to be torn to bits by a smarter player.

Nine-ball appears to be simplistic and lucky; after all, you blast the balls open on the game's opening break, and as long as you make contact with the lowest-numbered ball on the table first, anything else that goes in counts. But it's really a difficult, complex game of angles, with principles of position play unlike any other pool form; and like 8-ball, there are often situations that dictate your deliberately not making any balls.

We'll be taking a closer look at each of those games soon. The point I hope to leave you with here is a simple one, yet is overlooked by well over 90 percent of those who play pool at all: you absolutely have to recognize that *good pool has to do with far more than merely knocking balls into holes.* That perception alone definitely lends you the potential to improve, because all you really need to accommodate it are the same sound fundamentals you developed for shotmaking in the first place! We're working to change your *concept* of pool, not your execution of it.

A SMARTER WAY TO PRACTICE

While you've probably come across the old saw, "Practice makes perfect," pool, as usual, is a bit different. What's closer to the truth in pool is, "*Perfect* practice makes perfect."

The reason for that distinction is, very few pool players have a sound grasp of what productive practice really is, and most spend way too much time to accomplish way too little. I'm not minimizing the need for practice; not only do you need it, but you need a great, great deal of it. But your practice should be structured, so you can realize the optimal benefits from it.

Perhaps the most common error in pool practice is to simply roll the balls out loose on the table, and proceed to knock them into pockets. While there's nothing wrong with that on a limited basis, it's a grievous error to devote all your practice time to it; that's something like trying to turn your stretching exercises alone into a full-blown workout. Yes, sinking balls is where the fun is when it comes to pool, but the problem with shotmaking practice on a wide-open table is that it gives you almost no chance to correct anything.

Could there be a flaw in your stroke production? Pocketing open balls won't tell you. You will see plenty of misses if that's indeed the case, but you most likely will not know why.

Do certain kinds of shots give you more trouble than others? Then how do you hope to correct that imbalance with a wide-open table, which tempts you with all kinds of shots?

Is position play or shot selection your problem? You won't solve it through open-table shotmaking, which simply offers you a lot of easy shots with no particular reason for choosing one over the next.

Note that I'm not saying you should shun this form of practice entirely, only limit it. I use it myself as a preamble to something more disciplined, but I will generally roll out and sink the 15 balls no more than twice. This practice rack or two helps me tap into muscle memory, and, because it's easy, helps me set up a positive frame of mind. (The latter is critical if you expect to play well. If you're dwelling on negativity, for whatever reason, you don't belong at the pool table at all.)

Now let's consider some practice techniques that *will* help improve your game (why else practice at all?).

Practice with No Balls

The above subhead is not intended as a defamation of character. What it means instead is the same point we've already made repeatedly: your ability to play pool really boils down to your ability to bring the cue forward, in a perfectly straight line, to strike the cue ball in exactly the place you intended. It sounds simplistic, yet it's astounding how many ways *not* to do that players have figured out through the years.

This isn't tennis; there is only one basic stroke for you to learn. (Yes, many advanced players do have a number of variations on that stroke in their arsenals, but even those variations are produced with essentially the same basics.) And it isn't golf, either; a flawless pool stroke is elusive precisely because it's so simple, not because it's so complex (remember, in an ideal stroke the only moving body parts are the stroking forearm and the eyeballs). So what can you do to improve yours?

Any number of players still do the same thing they did in their first few days at the game: simply practice stroking an invisible ball atop the table's side rail. They don't spend very long at this, but it is a confidence builder, and the rail acts as a straightness check (in that if your stroke and follow-through are anything less than straight, your cue won't line up with the rail).

Several of today's top pros learned straight-stroke production with an empty pop bottle, practicing stroking into the bottle mouth without touching the sides (the handle of a coffee cup will serve the same purpose). Does it take an extra quotient of patience to stay with such a drill for more than a few minutes at a time? Yes. Will it pay off? An even more emphatic yes.

If you're willing to try this invaluable practice technique (good for you), do it justice. That means you should assume your best, most disciplined stance, and your firmest bridge, too. Don't get lazy on the exercise; you'll only be cheating yourself.

Practice with One Ball

As already noted, a fundamental mistake made by pool beginners is thinking the fate of the object balls is what pool is all about. Wrong. No matter what your pool game of choice, just about that entire game, and your potential success at it, resides in the cue ball.

Thus you really ought to plan on being good friends with that albino blob of plastic, and that begins mentally, not physically. Back in the early '70s, when sports psychology was just coming to the fore, a number of gurus actually recommended "loving" the ball of whatever sport you chose: basketball players learned to caress their ball's pebbly grain, tennis players learned to feel their ball's fuzz, pitchers groped every stitch of a baseball's seams, and so forth. While your cue ball boasts no such blemishes on its pristine surface, you can still train yourself to focus on its smoothness, its shiny finish, its little dot (if it has one; not all cue balls do), and so on. Many fine players develop the habit of looking for the reflection of their cue's tip in the cue ball's finish as they address it. And, of course, when you're successful at this type of absorption with the cue ball, what you're doing at the same time is shutting out distractions.

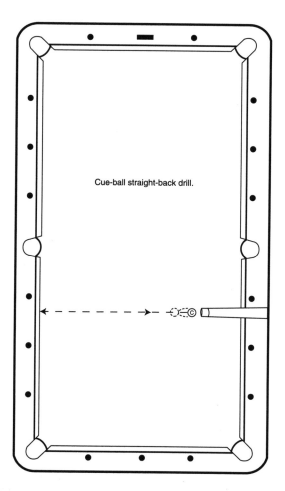

Diagram 16

Cue-ball straight-back drill.

You'd rather cue the ball than just sit there rhapsodizing about it? Fine. Then get to that table-spot drill we talked about in the "Your Stroke" section and check out your stroke's straightness and follow-through.

Has the table spot ceased to tattle on you (or, on the other hand, are you tired of its tattling)? Then try this drill. Stroke the cue ball to a rail perpendicularly (that is, your cue ball's line of travel to the rail is exactly a 90-degree angle to that rail). Again, freeze on your follow-through. A straight stroke and follow-through, plus a perfect center-ball hit on the cue ball, will bring the cue ball back to meet your cue tip

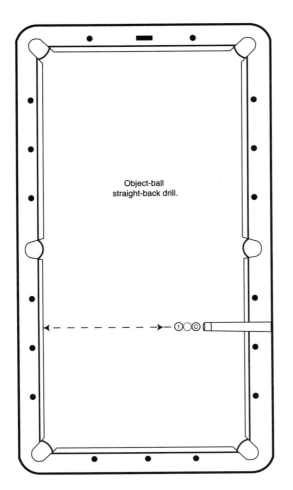

Diagram 17

Object-ball
straight-back drill.

where you followed through, as in Diagram 16. When you first get into this exercise, drive the ball at a side rail; as you become more proficient at it, drive the ball farther, to a short rail and back.

After your first few weeks at pool, by the way, none of these exercises should occupy more than a few minutes of your time—unless, of course, you hit a playing slump. In that unhappy case, every aspect of your game, beginning with your stroke-production fundamentals, should be examined. And the above drills, as simplistic as they might seem, can be terrific slump-busters.

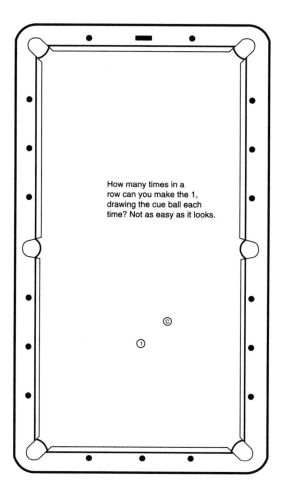

Diagram 18

How many times in a
row can you make the 1,
drawing the cue ball each
time? Not as easy as it looks.

Practice with Two Balls

How creative can you get with a cue ball and a single object ball?

The first tactic to try is promoting yourself from the cue-ball-back-to-cue-tip drill. Use the cue ball to drive your object ball to the rail instead, and try to make it return to contact the cue ball a second time (Diagram 17). Again, you must execute a straight stroke that contacts the cue ball at its vertical axis, plus an accurate object-ball hit, to bring this off.

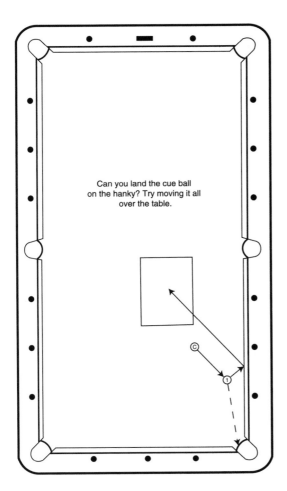

Diagram 19

Can you land the cue ball
on the hanky? Try moving it all
over the table.

Ready for something quite a bit tougher? Put the object ball on that big-mouthed table spot, and place the cue ball someplace where it forms a straight line with the object ball and any pocket (Diagram 18). Now see how many times in a row you can make the object ball in that same pocket, drawing the cue ball back to you each time and shooting from where it stops (anything over three is very, very good).

More practical than either of those two drills, in terms of aiding your own game, is to use that lone object ball to practice the shots you know give you trouble. Do you have a secret fear of shots with the object ball on or near a rail? Is cutting the ball thin a problem? (It is for most.) Do you need work on long shots? Bank shots? Straight-in shots? Now's your chance. If you can find the discipline to practice any given shot you don't like for 15 minutes or more, you should feel your comfort level with that shot increasing in your very first few practice sessions. (Another very good tip for overcoming your bugaboos on certain shots: set the shot up at the same angle that bothers you, but much closer to a pocket, a la the rail-shot examples of Diagrams 6 and 7. You should be able to increase the distance gradually in almost no time; once you're cured, make it a habit to visualize the pocket as being closer than it is.)

Another valuable technique that's been around at least since Willie Mosconi's timeless handbook from the '40s is to place a handkerchief somewhere on the table and try to make the cue ball come to rest there after pocketing something (Diagram 19). Move the hanky all over the table in trying this; it's a great way to learn table-area position.

Practice with Multiple Balls

The warm-up exercise we discussed at the beginning of this chapter, merely pocketing open balls, isn't a bad start. It's just that you don't want to make it the end-all, be-all of your practice. There isn't much challenge to it physically; neither does it allow you to tap into your mental abilities at pool, which are every bit as important as your physical ones.

Let's begin with a deceptively simple practice drill with two object balls. Roll those balls out on the table at random, but don't leave them close together. Now select a spot on the table for the cue ball where you can pocket the first of those balls reasonably easily *and* get acceptable position (say, within two feet of the object ball) on the second. When you can execute this drill without trouble 8 times out of 10, add a third object ball and work out a similar sequence. According to some of the teachers who endorse this drill, each object ball you can add to it represents close to a 50 percent improvement in your game!

Almost all top pool teachers agree that your typical practice session, once you have some familiarity with the various pool games, should include at least 30 minutes of straight pool. While the game has admittedly slipped in popularity (largely because its pace and occasional emphasis on defense are not especially TV-friendly), it's still the only form of pool that can teach you something about every other form. There are players, and good ones at that, who actually compete with themselves at this, even to the extent of playing defensive safeties on themselves (Irving Crane of Rochester, who played second fiddle to Willie Mosconi for most of his career but is still one of the all-time straight-pool greats, used to play himself safe for 30 minutes a day without fail. Now *that's* discipline!) I don't think you have to go quite that far; if you find yourself stymied and shotless, simply set up another break shot and begin another rack. Remember, one of the most important objectives of your practice is a positive outlook.

Diagram 20 suggests a typical break shot with which you might begin your straight-pool practice. When you hit this shot authoritatively, and with draw, you bring your cue ball back toward center table—the ideal place, because it maximizes your options—with, usually, four to seven object balls loose and the remainder still clustered. The idea of your practice should not be merely to see how many balls you can make in a row, but how well thought-out you can make your position sequences. Do not loaf just because you're practicing and not competing; take your firmest stance and your most disciplined bridge and grip, keep your head down, follow through, and so on.

Most players who are into good practice habits include some form of actual drills before they allow themselves the indulgence of straight pool. We've already considered one of the most common, the line of object balls halfway between a corner pocket and the cue ball (See Diagram 8 on page 43) and gradually increasing the distances from cue ball to object balls and object balls to pocket. Remember, both the halfway-between and the 8-out-of-10 aspects are key to this drill.

The L drill, shown in Diagram 21, is one of the most time-tested in the game; I'm not partial to it personally, but then I've never been

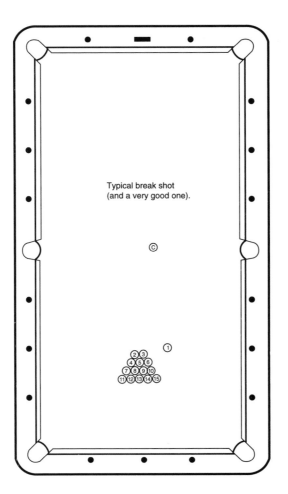

Diagram 20

terribly good with it. You start by shooting in the ball closest to the end rail, striving for position on the next ball in line using draw on your cue ball. Expert players frequently increase the difficulty of the drill by not allowing the cue ball to touch a rail, but let's allow you the use of that bottom rail for now. Anything over six or seven balls in a row in this drill is quite good indeed, and if you stay with this, you will benefit from heightened touch and control of cue-ball speed, especially with your draw stroke. Incidentally, to keep you encouraged, once you get past the seven balls leading away from the bottom rail, the last eight will probably be easier to knock off.

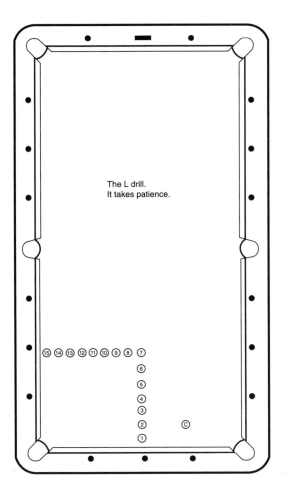

Diagram 21

The L drill.
It takes patience.

The circle drill shown in Diagram 22 isn't quite as parochial as the L drill; you may take the balls in any order you wish. What you may *not* do is allow your cue ball to stray outside the circle. It's another way of improving your use of draw, but now you're sending the object balls a greater distance than you do in the L.

Much more rarely seen is the long line of Diagram 23, down the center of the length of the table. The idea is to start with the eighth, or center, ball in line, pocketing it in a corner pocket and drawing your cue ball back just far enough that you can pocket the next ball in line going the opposite direction, and so on. As you continue to pocket

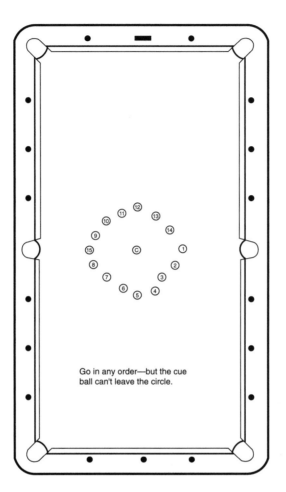

Diagram 22

Go in any order—but the cue
ball can't leave the circle.

these balls, the interval between them obviously increases; thus you
must draw the cue ball farther and farther each time. It takes a real
player to knock off the entire line, but stay with this. It'll pay off.

Somewhat similar to that is the layout of Diagram 24. There was
a time, way, way back, when straight pool was actually played like
this; when each player's turn ended, all the balls that player had sunk
were respotted in a line behind the spot where the head ball goes at the
start of the game. If the player ran all 15 balls, the balls were re-lined
up just as you see in the diagram, hence the name "lineup pool." Its use
to you today is to improve your touch, position, and especially your

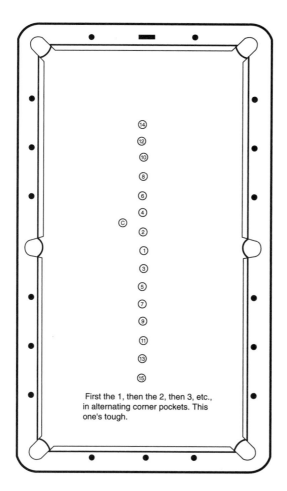

Diagram 23

First the 1, then the 2, then 3, etc., in alternating corner pockets. This one's tough.

finesse-draw shots. To save time, use two cues to help you line the balls up straight. You begin with the ball nearest the bottom rail, and play position for the next succeeding balls in line; at some point after the third ball or so, you're going to have to play position for a shot that lets you pocket one while loosening some others instead of just picking them off cleanly.

One of the last drills I usually execute before beginning my straight-pool practice (or competition, for that matter) is the three-ball exercise you see in Diagram 25. The idea is to make all three balls in the same side pocket, using draw on the cue ball and without sending it to a rail.

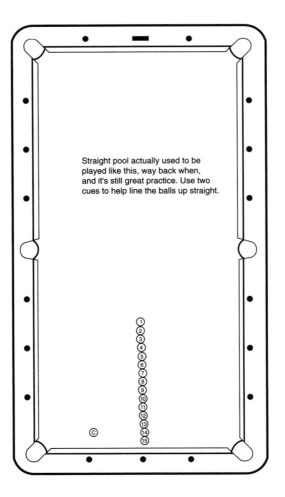

Diagram 24

Straight pool actually used to be played like this, way back when, and it's still great practice. Use two cues to help line the balls up straight.

It's not quite as easy as it looks, and it does get you in touch with all the feelings of pool: stance, grip, bridge, stroke, pocketing, and position. Again, this is exactly analogous to the golfer who warms up with short putts instead of long drives.

Finally, if you just can't wean yourself from the habit of rolling the balls out on the table loose, here are two more tough, creative, and highly useful drills in that format.

1. See how many shots you can make in a row without having your cue ball touch any ball other than the one you pocket.

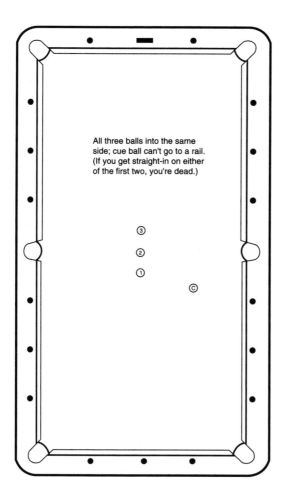

Diagram 25

All three balls into the same side; cue ball can't go to a rail. (If you get straight-in on either of the first two, you're dead.)

2. See how many shots you can make in a row without having your cue ball touch a rail.

The second is considerably harder than the first, but either or both will do wonders for your position play. When you can combine them—that is, clear the table without touching a second object ball or going to a rail—you will have truly achieved intermediate status, and will be eminently ready for bigger and better things.

Do you need to include all the above drills in your practice? Not necessarily. It couldn't hurt, but my own practice is more brief than that, so I'd suggest you pick and choose according to what seems to help most if you don't have the time or patience for the whole megillah. Here's what I typically do:

1. Fire four or five balls directly into a corner pocket, using most of the diagonal length of the table. It's an extremely simple stroke warm-up.

2. The object-balls-halfway drill. I usually begin with a four-diamonds-to-two ratio, then five-to-two-and-a-half, ending at six-to-three. If things are going particularly well, I might continue to seven-to-three-and-a-half. But I stop at the point where I'm no longer sinking 8 out of the line of 10.

3. The three-balls-into-the-same-side-pocket drill, only till I execute it correctly once.

4. Balls loose on a table, trying not to let the cue ball touch a second object ball after pocketing the one I aimed at. Two racks maximum.

5. Anywhere from half a rack to a full rack of balls left-handed (my opposite hand).

6. Straight-pool practice. Actually, I'm capable of doing this for great stretches at a time, and frequently do just that when there's no competition available. But you be content with 30 minutes or more. It's nice—in fact, it's the ultimate reward—to make many balls consecutively in this phase of practice. But the real objective is to get you *thinking* good pool before you attempt to play it. Even if you run no more than five or six, it's a worthwhile endeavor if that run was correctly planned and executed. My total time invested in most precompetition practice sessions is 45 minutes to an hour. It sounds like quite a bit, but it goes by quickly; and besides, as I mentioned, I need close to half that time just to get loose at the table anyway. Disaster awaits if I try to compete with any less warm-up or practice than that.

There isn't a professional musician alive who didn't have to practice scales at some point, and the objectives of such practice are considerably more ambitious than the mere mastering of do-re-mi-fa, and so on. Your pool practice is no different. Is it as much fun as playing the game? No. Can you become any kind of player without it? To be as honest with you as I can, some very gifted and lucky competitors don't seem to need it, but they're a tiny minority. I'm on much safer ground, at least statistically, when I say you're going to need your practice. That's why it's so essential that it be the right kind of practice.

A SMARTER APPROACH TO
PLAYING POSITION

In golf, since you're playing against a score rather than a formal opponent as such, you get as many consecutive turns as you need. In
Monopoly, and a few other board games, you can get a second consecutive turn if the dice roll favorably. But with those few exceptions,
pool remains the world's only game to offer you unlimited consecutive
turns as long as you can execute.

And with that in mind, you might as well learn the game so as to
afford yourself longer and longer stretches at the table. In your first few
weeks at the game, there is very little question that when you play, the
better shotmaker between you and your opponent will win. Should
that happen to be you, it's absolutely mandatory that you resist the
temptation to rest on those puny laurels. The same shotmaking ability
that helps you knock off your neophyte peers with regularity will do
you minimal good when you start taking on better competition—and
if you're serious about improving, you should make it a point to find
the very stiffest competition you can; if you need some sort of handicap to make the game fair, fine.

Naturally, I do not advocate betting the mortgage in competition
with champions; but within the limits of common sense, I have no
moral qualms about suggesting that you wager a few bob on yourself.
This is not an argument in favor of gambling per se; it's just that a modest bet will go a long way toward improving your focus and helping you

stand up to the game's pressures. (The theory is that any shot you can execute properly with your cash on the line, you certainly ought to be able to replicate in a tournament or for fun.)

More to the point, by seeking out more advanced players, you avail yourself of the opportunity to see how position should be played. And that should be a learning experience; sitting in the chair fuming while your opponent hands you your head teaches you very little, except possibly not to play that opponent again. In fact, without some understanding of the principles of correct position play, the chances are excellent that you will not be able to figure out exactly why your opponent can string shots together so much better than you. If your answer is simply, "He just shoots better," that *could* be right, but it's much more likely that he understands some things that you don't. Yet.

Shall we begin catching up?

Naturally, your position requirements will vary considerably from pool game to pool game. In straight pool (and only in straight pool), you may theoretically attempt to shoot any ball into any pocket at any point in the game. In 8-ball, of the 15 object balls on the table, no more than 7 will be legal targets for you once the stripes/solids commitment has been made, frequently less. In 9-ball, the only legal target you may begin with is the lowest-numbered ball on the table. And still, for all that diversity (which we'll address in the chapters on the specific games), there are still some position-play rules of thumb that apply across the board.

Pool's Two Types of Shots

All pool shots can be categorized in one of two ways: those in which you can predict your cue ball's final resting place with absolute certainty, and those in which you cannot. Obviously, the second category outweighs the first many, many times over. Just as obviously, the first category is largely composed of those shots in which you either stop the cue ball dead or limit its travel to just a few inches.

Be advised here and now, however, that no one's book, mine or anyone else's, is going to teach you how to go about driving the cue ball a precise desired distance. That is strictly a matter of feel, and in playing pool successfully, feel (or "touch") ranks second only to eyesight among your critical senses. Feel comes with experience and confidence.

While we're on this subject, by the way, hearing is a vastly underrated and underutilized sense when it comes to pool. Every successful pool shot has three distinct sounds (and unsuccessful shots have just two): the tap of your cue tip against the cue ball; the click of cue ball meeting object ball; and the plop of an object ball falling into a pocket. The intervals between these sounds will vary from shot to shot, obviously, but there are some nifty benefits of teaching yourself to anticipate, and listen for, the cadence of those sounds. It goes a long, long way toward shutting out mental interference.

Area Position Play

Because of the unpredictability of most shots, as mentioned above, most of the time your position-play objective should be an *area* of the table, not a specific spot. Now and then, the table layouts you face will offer you teeny-weeny areas for your cue ball to visit, and scorn you when you cannot, but that's part of the game. Trying to play nothing less than pinpoint position is a nice way to make yourself bonkers. Perfection will come naturally enough during those magical interludes when you really hit your stride, without your having to will it in the slightest way. For now, do both of us a favor and accept the concept of table-area position, with this one critical qualifier: *you must learn to distinguish between merely having a next shot available and real position playing.* The former might bail you out of some sticky wickets on a short-term basis (or it might not; nobody makes everything); over the long term, the latter camp is where you want to be.

The Advantages of Angled Shots

This principle would seem to oppose the predictable-vs.-unpredictable-shots concept that we've already discussed, but it's irrefutable: position play will come to you far more easily once you understand that shots delineating a modest angle between cue ball, object ball, and pocket are, most of the time, considerably more beneficial than shots that form a straight line, especially in 8-ball and 9-ball. Even though your cue ball's ultimate stopping place is harder to predict, the fact remains that angled shots (cut shots) offer you many, many more options for cue-ball travel. When you have a cut shot, in theory you can send the cue ball just about anyplace on the table; when you have a straight-in shot, the cue ball is clearly going to end up on the same line you began with, or very close, unless you draw it all the way back to a rail and then out again.

Secondary Object Balls

In all forms of pool, you simply must learn the desirability of pocketing a single ball without disturbing any others—unless there's a purpose to doing so. All pool games, especially straight pool, will confront you with situations that combine open, obvious shots with clusters that must be altered or separated before any of the clustered balls can be negotiated. Accordingly, you'll have to master shots in which your cue ball dismantles a cluster after pocketing a ball (*break shots*, as they're called). But *you never want to move a second object ball that is already pocketable.* This is one of the key premises of all intermediate-or-better pool. The reason: if you turn your cue ball loose to run willy-nilly into one or more open object balls, how are you going to predict its destination? (Or that of the balls you run into, for that matter?) And if you can't predict its destination, how are you going to play position?

There is no way to count the number of pool games that have turned around completely because the shooter accidentally nudged a second object ball, even if trivially. You *must* learn this.

Rail Shots

In pool games that offer you a choice of shots (in other words, just about any form of pool except 9-ball or its ancestor, "rotation"), you should strive to shoot balls that rest on—or very close to—a rail sooner rather than later. Rail shots are frequently intimidating to student players, but there are two good reasons to practice them. In the first place, you may well need the rails clear for future cue-ball travels (and remember, from a mental perspective, pool is simply a matter of looking ahead). Second, when you leave object balls on the rail with clusters yet to be broken elsewhere on the table, you risk creating more miniclusters with your subsequent break shots, and simply trading one problem for another one without really solving either.

In fact, rail shots are just one example of why you should deal with problems early on instead of letting them go (in pool as well as in life). When you confront a layout offering both open shots and clustered balls that must be separated, your plan should begin with, *Where are the trouble spots, and how am I going to deal with them?*

A Rail-Shot Exception

One important exception to the principle just discussed: in both straight pool and 8-ball, it will pay dividends to leave one ball—but only one—on the bottom rail until all the other balls are open, as in Diagram 26. The theory is that in case you are unlucky in separating the remaining clustered balls and your cue ball ends up down there, you'll be terribly grateful for the company.

Clear the Corner Pockets

In straight pool, the two corner pockets nearest where the balls are racked to begin with are really the lion's share of the game; good straight-pool players will pocket close to 85 or 90 percent of their shots there. Accordingly, learn to look for balls that, once sunk, will clear the way to those two pockets for other balls (Diagram 27). And, once again, take those balls off earlier in your sequence, not later; that good habit will afford you many more options as you go along.

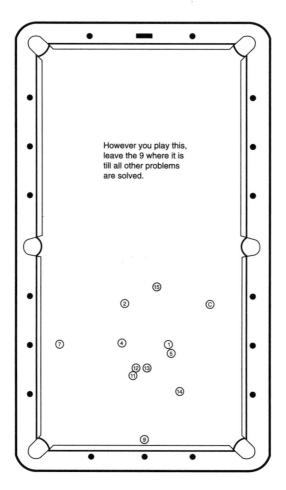

Diagram 26

However you play this,
leave the 9 where it is
till all other problems
are solved.

In 8-ball, the same principle applies, except that the balls for which you're attempting to clear the way should be yours (or the 8, if you're en route to winning the game outright); there's no point to clearing a path for your opponent's balls unless you see a way to keep him from getting back to the table at all.

Keep It Simple

More often than you'd think, the correct position option is a quite simple one. Every complexity you add, in the form of spin on the ball or

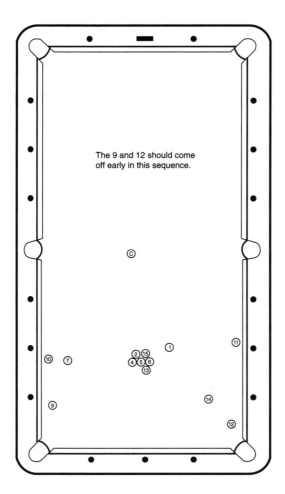

Diagram 27

The 9 and 12 should come off early in this sequence.

rails in its route, makes it that much more difficult to predict its destination. Accordingly, don't use sidespin unless it's functional for you, as previously discussed; and don't use more rails than you need to. If you can deliver the cue ball someplace desirable by sending it off one rail, don't use two. If a one-rail or two-rail route will get the job done, don't use three, and so on.

Your two most conspicuous exceptions to the above are worth mentioning. All pool games, but especially 8-ball and 9-ball, will offer you layouts with an object ball on or near a short rail where the cue ball must be sent toward the opposite end of the table. Almost all advanced

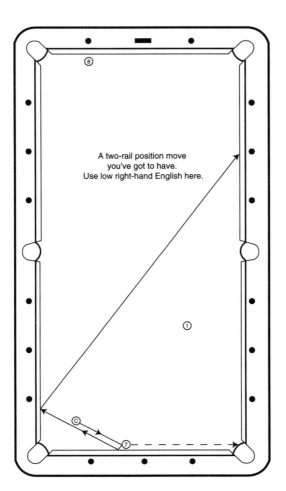

Diagram 28

A two-rail position move
you've got to have.
Use low right-hand English here.

players, assuming they have some angle to the shot to work with, will opt to bring the cue ball out of there using two rails in preference to one—especially when the object ball in question lies within a ball's width of the rail. (See Diagram 28.) The shot usually requires outside draw (that is, cueing the ball low on the side opposite to the direction of the object ball; low right-hand English for the shot that sends the object ball to the left, and vice-versa), and the shooter has to both provide sufficient speed and get his cue out of the cue ball's way in time, but that's the preferred way to play such a shot. (Very good players frequently select cue-ball routes off one or more rails that send the ball over the table's exact middle; any cue ball crossing that point cannot possibly scratch.)

Second, and especially in straight pool and 8-ball, proper position play will often require you to *look beyond the obvious* (for example, the ball closest to the ball you're shooting now is not necessarily your correct next shot). This would seem to defy the logic of choosing simple position solutions, but it really doesn't; you're still well-advised to stay in the cue ball's vertical center, minimize your use of rails, avoid touching secondary object balls that are already pocketable, and so on. Looking beyond the obvious simply means that you may have to send your cue ball a bit farther for optimal position than the immediate layout would suggest.

Playing the Center

The end rails of a pool table host three decorative diamonds each. Visualize the center-table area between the first and third diamonds, as in Diagram 29. A number of top players play position, especially in 9-ball, by keeping their cue ball within that area, straying from it only when absolutely necessary. That technique helps ensure that most shots will be angled; even more certainly, it ensures that the player will be confronted with a minimal number of shots off a rail.

How Far Ahead?

While you may have heard of players who were said to plan the entire table in advance once the balls were loose, that's my idea of inviting the guys with butterfly nets into your life. Willie Mosconi, perhaps the finest player who ever lived, claimed to plan position six shots ahead, but it's fair to presume his mental abilities were the equal of his physical ones, which were peerless.

The fact is, if you can consistently plan three shots in advance, you will be playing pool correctly and well. The three-shot planning pro-

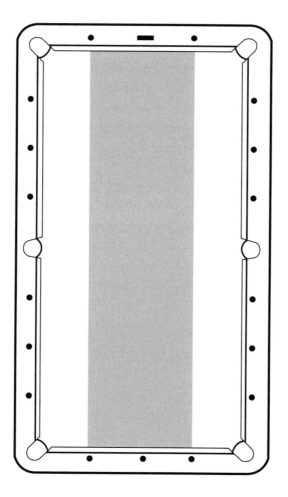

Diagram 29

cess will vary somewhat from one form of pool to another, once again, but its core consists of these questions:

a. Which ball do I want next after the one I'm shooting?

b. Which ball do I want after that?

c. About where do I want to stop the cue ball for my shot on ball (a) so that I can get decent position on ball (b)?

Discipline yourself to ask these questions, and provide the answers, on each shot, and I can promise you exciting progress. If they seem simple to you, great; by far, your biggest obstacles in position play are confusion and intimidation, and a simple weapon with which to take them on, and create order out of chaos, should do wonders for your attitude.

So as not to overwhelm you, we'll limit the position guidelines to these for now, and explore the nuances of position in the various pool games in the chapters to follow. Remember, position play is nothing to fear or allow to discourage you; on the contrary, solving and executing the position problems you face are where most of the game's fulfillment lies. (In my opinion, anyway, some players simply get their jollies winning the cash; I have no problem with that, but they don't know what they're missing.) Pool will offer you all sorts of clues (including false ones), codes to crack, and secret passageways to explore, and making all that work in your favor is good for a very special glow indeed. If you find you like these mind-game, problem-solving aspects of pool (and I have very little doubt you will) and want some more practice at it, my book *How Would You Play This?* deals with that subject exclusively.

A SMARTER APPROACH TO STRAIGHT POOL

This is the grande dame of all pool games. It has admittedly, and sadly, slipped in popularity among top players, for a number of barely relevant reasons: its defensive aspects are not particularly TV-friendly; it fosters very little gambling action (the games that do—principally 9-ball, one-pocket, and bank pool—are all but senseless to play *except* for money); and it has ceased to be the tournament staple, in part because 9-ball is the only pool game to be seen on cable TV.

Its importance to you as a pool beginner, however, is not diminished in the least. Straight pool remains far and away the best teaching basis from which to become competitive, no matter what your pool preference turns out to be. (Oddly, among advanced players, the opposite is true; it's pretty well-documented that an accomplished 9-ball player will pick up straight pool way before the reverse takes place, in part because the 9-ball player is far more used to complex shots and position patterns. But for where you are now, this is the ideal beginning.)

The game's optimal value to you is in helping you learn correct pool *choices*. No other form of pool permits you to attempt any ball into any pocket at any point in the game. In 8-ball, you need pocket a maximum of just eight balls to win; in 9-ball, there aren't even 15 balls to begin with, and only one of them counts toward winning. It wouldn't be much of a stretch to conclude that with all those balls available, plus the freedom to shoot any ball anywhere, straight pool is the easiest game, but it would be a mathematical oversimplification and dead wrong. That rich smorgasbord of choices makes straight pool one very challenging endeavor.

Let's begin by once more separating all straight-pool shots (excluding your defensive ones; we're coming to that too) into two categories: those in which you pocket a ball cleanly without disturbing the remainder of the table layout, and those in which your cue ball must move one or more object balls in addition to the one you sink. That is basically what straight pool is about. Yes, you pocket balls, but at the same time you see to it that all the remaining balls become pocketable too. Since straight pool is the game's only form requiring transitions from one rack to the next, the most important example of this concept is your ability to leave the last ball of each rack someplace where you can both pocket it and separate at least some of the remaining 14 clustered balls. But each individual rack figures to confront you with the same challenge in microcosm. Straight-pool break shots in which you separate a 14-ball cluster completely, with no further layout alterations necessary, are not as common as you might think.

I don't propose to delve into your lifestyle, but assuming you were responsibly raised, you'll recognize a number of parallels between playing pool correctly and mature decisionmaking in the rest of your life. In pool, you correctly deal with problems sooner rather than later; you recognize that certainties are far more valuable than probabilities; when you're forced to take a risk, and the game will certainly confront you with that demand many times over, you'll do much better if you acknowledge all your options and calculate your chances and the probable rewards or consequences. Is life so different?

The position guidelines we looked at in the last chapter are all demonstrated best by straight pool. But let's look at the game's aspects in the order in which they confront you.

The Opening Break

Almost every beginners' book extant has offered instruction on how the balls should be broken to start the game, and I frankly don't have many embellishments to add to that particular instruction. Most players will place the cue ball at or near a point in line with the outside diamond on the short rail and the second diamond up from that rail (although some begin from a position closer to the side rail than that). Most players will also add a bit of sidespin to the cue ball to help guard against a scratch in the corner diagonally opposite to where the cue ball contacts the stack. (In other words, if the cue ball is placed to the right of the racked balls as the player faces them, he would strike the cue ball maybe one cue tip northeast of its exact middle; if the cue ball is to the left, one cue tip northwest.) Your correct point of aim on the corner ball in the rack is that point at which it is in line with the rest of the row; in a perfect break, that corner ball and the ball at the other end of the rear line are the only ones that will move, and they will return to their original racked position or very close, but perfect breaks are extremely rare. In order to complete a legal straight-pool break, you must drive at least two object balls to a rail, and most of the time you'll loosen something else too. That's why it's important to get the cue ball all the way back to the opposite end rail, to make those loose object balls as challenging to shoot at as you can. Distance is a great equalizer in all forms of pool, and is one of the primary guidelines to playing defense (we're coming to that, too).

Playing the Game

Now let's take a look at a game situation, and examine how to apply what you've already learned. Almost every rack of straight pool will involve all your position guidelines, or at least most of them. By the way, these analyses tend to become wordy, but don't be intimidated by that. Bear with me, and let me reassure you that pool decisions take just a few seconds to make, once you're used to making them, even if it does take longer than that to read about them.

We've already agreed not to think of shots in terms of "harder" or "easier"; after all, unless an object ball is in a can't-miss position on the very edge of a pocket, your point of aim is pretty much the same size

Diagram 30

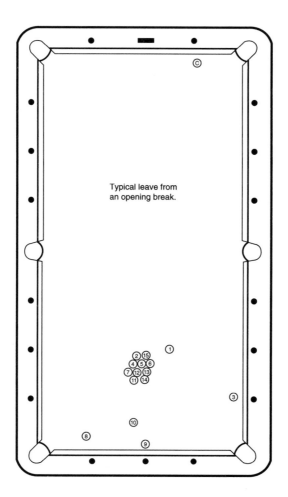

Typical leave from
an opening break.

for all shots. Still, unless you're a very unusual beginner indeed, your comfort level with pool's various shots is going to be bouncing like a kangaroo until you have some experience. So we'll factor that into the equation too—for now. As you progress, you'll soon learn that you just cannot choose the simplest solution every single time, because that will not always be the right choice.

Diagram 30 shows you a fairly typical leave from an opening break in straight pool. Most of the balls are still clustered, with some loose, and undoubtedly you'll identify one or more of the open object balls as shots you'd like to take on in preference to others. That approach is already incorrect; your decision should ideally be based on your analysis of which shot makes the most sense, rather than which one scares you the least. Still, you're well-advised to "play within yourself," just as in all sports, and it's senseless to select a shot in which you have little or no confidence unless you're really facing no other options.

Thus the 1 ball, nearest the clustered balls, presents something of a dilemma, even though it's only your very first turn in the game. Among advanced players, who have overcome their shotmaking fear (a very, *very* large step in a player's development), some would go for the 1 immediately; others would opt to get the cue ball closer to the 1 first by using other open shots to achieve the desired position.

The reasoning of the first group goes like this: If I make it, I'll splatter most or all of the remaining clustered balls, and will have a good chance of running the rack and getting off to a good lead. If I should miss, there's still a chance—not quite as unlikely as it seems—that I'll get lucky and not leave many, or even any, good shots. And even if I miss and do leave open shots, there's still the possibility that my opponent will mess up and take less than full advantage of my gaffe.

Meanwhile, the second group formulates a plan like this: Those open balls other than the 1 are of no particular use to me later in the rack. If I choose the 1 now, and break open some or all of the remaining cluster, I'll be driving object balls toward those that are already open, creating the possibility of more miniclusters for me to deal with. Besides, some of the open shots I have now are on or close to rails, and I want those rails open for later in my shot sequence. The 1 will work just as efficiently for me two or three shots from now, assuming I achieve desirable position closer to it.

While I can't fault the first group's reasoning, and am frankly deeply jealous of their fearlessness, the second group's thinking is easier to support, at least intellectually. Of course it's exhilarating, to say nothing of hideously intimidating, to fire in a long break shot and treat your opponent to a good long stay "in the chair" right at the outset of a game, but pool is best played in the complete absence of emotion. The most dangerous players are those whose expressions and behavior offer no clue whatsoever as to how the game might be going—a quality you'd do well to emulate. Emotional displays in any direction only serve as a distraction to yourself; if you're the type who rattles or angers easily, that is just what a smart opponent will be waiting to see. If you rejoice prematurely and/or unduly at the favorable way things are going, you will only dilute your focus upon the business at hand and lower your performance.

So let's put you in that second camp, for now. But before we proceed, correctly or any other way, there's another nuance of the game we need to consider: reading the stack. Of pool's three major forms, straight pool is the only one where the game begins with a finesse break that deliberately does *not* demolish the rack. (The game known as one-pocket does, too, but that extremely difficult game is inappropriate for a beginners' book; and besides, it is too complex to do justice in a single chapter.) Since most of the rack remains more or less intact after a good straight-pool break, those clustered balls will frequently offer you a free gift in the form of a shot that cannot be missed. These are called *dead* shots. Oddly, and for reasons I've never been able to fathom, shots that cannot possibly be made are called *stiffs*. While the two terms are interchangeable in everyday jargon, obviously you'll have to learn the distinction, and well, when it comes to pool. We've already taken a look at the major delightful varieties of these, the combination and the carom, in the section entitled "The Other Shots" in Chapter 1. The best straight-pool players elevate reading the stack to an art form, uncovering shots the average competitor would never dream of.

Because there's a very subtle line between shots out of a cluster that can be made and those that cannot, they tend to defy precise diagramming, but I've given you the correct general guidelines in the section on shotmaking. *You should inspect clustered balls every single time you come to the table to begin your turn, and after each time a cluster has been altered in the slightest way.* Even the most subtle change can change an impossible shot into a beginner's delight. For now, though, let's say you've found no dead-shot possibilities; further, as suggested, you're in the second, more conservative group of players described above. Here's how you'd proceed, utilizing what we've already discussed:

Make a Plan

As Elaine said to Benjamin in *The Graduate*, "I don't want you to leave without a plan." Do not aim any shots, or begin to assume your stance and form your bridge, without a sensible strategy for acquiring good position. Of the balls that are open in Diagram 30, you already know to leave one on or near the bottom rail until all remaining problems are solved. Since the 9 is seated so symbolically right smack-dab in the middle of that rail, let's agree that will be our "insurance" or "safety-valve" ball. So all that's left is to estimate how far your cue ball will roll past the 3 when you play that ball, and make a plan that uses the 8 and 10, in either order, to get good center-table position on the 1, from where you can attack the clustered balls. If the cue ball rolls too far (or not far enough) to make your original plan viable, that's when you improvise. In this example, even if you wound up straight-in on either the 8 or 10, position for a next shot would still present little problem, although a modest angle on each would be preferable. Generally, I believe strongly in sticking with your original plan as long as it seems feasible; otherwise you begin second-guessing far too many of your choices, losing your playing rhythm and your confidence right with it.

As you can see, it would also be possible to attack the clustered balls from the rear, using the 10. Let's consider the pros and cons of that choice. Mike Sigel, a Billiard Congress of America hall-of-famer and winner of more major titles than any pool player in history, actually seeks out break-shot patterns such as this; his reasoning is that since the center of the table is open, that's a desirable area to send object balls. Further, such opportunities almost always exist early in a rack of straight pool; break shots from the front or side of the rack, such as the 1, may not. If the 1 were closer to the rack than it is now, rendering it unplayable, you'd *have* to work toward from-the-rear break-shot position.

But in this case you do have a choice, and here are the arguments in favor of breaking a cluster from in front or to the side. First, unless you drastically overhit your break shot, you tend to keep the open object balls down at the business end of the table, and thus your cue ball needs to travel less. Second, center table is your number-one choice for the *cue* ball, for maximum position options, and you won't be able to utilize center table nearly as well if you've already scattered some object balls there. And third, from-the-rear break shots carry pitfalls of their own. You're attacking the cluster at its broadest point, with the mass of most of the clustered balls behind that point—hence the balls will be more difficult to separate. Equally important, you don't want to keep your cue ball back there, because you'll be too far from the newly open object balls; that means that your from-the-rear break shot either must contact the corner ball in the back row, or travel a complex three-rail route between the broken balls and the bottom rail, to have any chance at all of ending up with something reasonably short for you to shoot.

Re-Breaking the Balls

Diagram 31 assumes we used the 8 and 10 advantageously to get position on the 1, and made it with these results. You now want a reasonable idea of where your cue ball will travel after contacting the clustered balls. (You obviously can't plan three shots ahead when your break ball is the only remaining open shot, unless you're Kreskin, thus it becomes more important than ever to at least anticipate what the cue ball will do.) It is not enough to determine simply that your cue ball will contact the cluster and let things go at that. First you want to determine exactly what point of that cluster will be contacted. Ideally, that will be a corner ball in the cluster, because corner balls are open on one side, granting you access to unoccupied space for the cue ball. What you clearly don't want is to separate some balls out of the cluster but leave

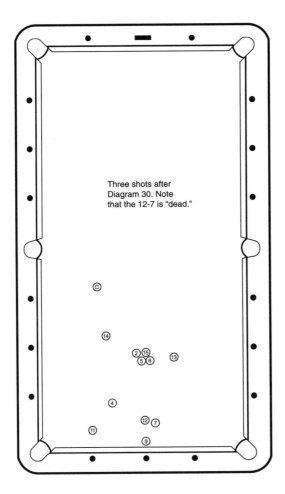

Diagram 31

Three shots after
Diagram 30. Note
that the 12-7 is "dead."

the cue ball stuck on some others, and that happens most often when
the cue ball contacts a clustered ball sandwiched between others rather
than a corner ball. If your break shot lies so that the cue ball simply
must take on one of those interior balls first, then some extra speed and
draw (rather than follow) on the cue ball are definitely both advised.

The 1 ball in the diagram, however, allowed us to contact one of
the top balls in the stack, and that is desirable. Remember, however,
that your first objective on most break shots—besides pocketing the
break ball and opening up at least some of the others—should be to get
the cue ball to center table. For that reason, it is rarely a good idea to

hit your break shots with follow, sending your cue ball in the same direction as the broken balls; it's far too easy to get the cue ball tied up that way. Drawing the cue ball, to bring it back toward you counter to the direction of the object balls now in motion, is usually a much wiser choice. And because you'll be contacting the top of the stack here, you don't even have to do that. A dead-center hit on the cue ball will serve you well on shots like the 1; just remember to use sufficient speed to drive the cue ball clear of the clustered ball you strike with it.

Opening All the Balls

Here, in Diagram 31, are the results of your secondary break shot, having successfully pocketed the 1. Predictably, there is still some work to be done; the four object balls still clustered must be moved somehow; but with that few balls, they don't need to be moved far, and can in fact be finessed apart rather than blasted to kingdom come. Because the 12-7 tandem is dead into the corner pocket, you have an easy, natural approach to nudging that cluster apart. Note that the 13 would be an excellent ball to leave as your break shot into the next rack; unfortunately, that may not be possible here, because you have only one other open shot, the 14, which figures to move the 13 anyway, and besides would leave you with way too many object balls near the bottom rail. No use fretting about not being able to save the 14; the game will deny you that way all the time. So use the 14 to get to the 4, and from the 4 you should be able to achieve a reasonable angle on the 12-7 combination, which should be a cinch to make, gently separating those last four balls at the same time.

Proceeding with All Balls Open

In Diagram 32, all the balls are open after pocketing the 7. At this point in the rack—and not before—you formulate a position plan that includes both that last ball you've been saving on the bottom rail, and the ball you'd like to save as your break shot for the next rack (in

Diagram 32

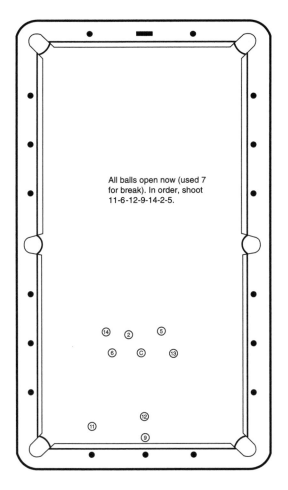

All balls open now (used 7
for break). In order, shoot
11-6-12-9-14-2-5.

straight pool, as you probably know, the balls are reracked in a 14-ball cluster when one object ball remains on the table; some of the typical break shots you should strive for are covered in the next section). As diagrammed, your best possibility for your next-rack break shot is the 13, so let's plan around that ball. The 5, just above the 13, is ideal to save for next-to-last (such a shot is commonly referred to as a "key" ball), because it lies right where you'd want the cue ball to be if you were shooting the 13. So, working backward from those two balls, a workable plan would go like this.

The "Three Shots Ahead" Concept

Start with the 11, which you were saving as a safety valve from your 7-ball secondary break shot anyway. With all the balls open, you should be able to implement your "three shots ahead" formula now, as well as the rule of tangents and the concept of table-area position. While the 9 and 12 seem like logical next shots after the 11, the 6 is really not a bad choice either. You have a natural angle to enter a desirable area of the table (shaded) for position on it (see Diagram 33); besides, the 2 and 14, as situated, hinder you in getting to it from center table. Following that thinking (and an open layout such as this admittedly could be negotiated in several ways), you'd have decided something like, *"My next shot is the 6, the shot after that is the 12, and here's where I want to be on the 6 to get to the 12,"* and your eventual sequence could go 11-6-12-9-14(probably in the far corner; you must always inspect your layouts from all directions—after all, all six pockets count equally)-2-5 in the near side pocket, maybe the other far corner depending on your exact angle, for good break position on the 13.

And that's how you'd go about "running the table" correctly in straight pool. Of course I understand that it's not particularly realistic to expect you to bring off a run like this early in your development at the game, even if the printed page does make it seem easy (although it will be attainable sooner than you think, if you apply yourself the right way). The idea is simply to get you *thinking* good pool early; that's by far your best chance to see your good playing following closely behind.

Less-than-ideal shot selection has stymied many a decent shot-maker. An improper shot sequence, no matter how adept you might be at pocketing balls, will lead to your turning the cue ball loose for too many flights that are impossible to chart. At that point, you'll be trusting luck, and little else, to provide you with open shots to continue your run; making a lot of shots consecutively is mostly a matter of being able to predict your cue ball's final resting place, which is far, far easier when you choose the right shots to play. Learning correct position play is far more complex than learning shotmaking basics—and I say that for your benefit, not to intimidate you. You should be able to make shots

Diagram 33

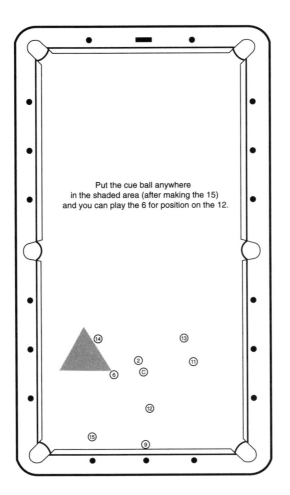

Put the cue ball anywhere
in the shaded area (after making the 15)
and you can play the 6 for position on the 12.

with some consistency within a few weeks, maybe sooner, depending on your natural aptitude for the game, how often and diligently you practice and/or play, and how well you utilize proper fundamentals. But how long it will take you to achieve a grasp of position-play basics is considerably less predictable. Some naturals pick it up right away (an ability with what your high-school aptitude tests called *spatial relations* helps considerably; what it specifically does is permit the player to perceive which balls go with which others, in formulating a sequence); some have to work harder to become competent at it; some never conquer their bad position habits, not even after years and years. There is no apparent reason why you, having had the marvelous sense to come to this book, should join the latter group. Just be disciplined and calm about formulating sensible position plans for each shot; it's all too easy not to exhibit either of those qualities.

The 11 you've left yourself for a break shot is a good one; not only will your cue ball contact the stack if you sink the 11, but you'll contact it at its corner, as advised. Let's take a look at some other common break shots that the game will give you an opportunity to strive for.

Common Straight-Pool Break Shots

First, let's agree that you have to watch for object balls in these locations well before you're ever ready to use them as break shots. I've already given you one of position play's cardinal rules—don't move object balls that are already open. But few straight-pool sins are as heinous as moving an object ball that would have been a good break ball. To avoid that sin and the damnation that inevitably follows, the first step is to recognize their potential.

Second, be aware that break shots threaten to diffuse your focus. You're concentrating on pocketing a ball, taking on the stack, and getting your cue ball free, all at the same time. And that makes it all too easy to forget about the rule of tangents, which is especially critical on your break shots because it helps you *predict exactly which ball in the rack your cue ball will strike first*. Striking a corner ball in the stack rather than an interior one is so important to your successful execution that it's well worth cueing the ball someplace other than you ordinarily would to achieve it. The balls *can* be broken successfully by running into interior balls instead of a corner one, but it usually requires extra speed and entails extra risks.

The break shot of Diagram 34 is about as good as it gets. You'll be taking on the top ball in the stack; solid draw and no more than medium cue-ball speed should bring the cue ball right back to center table. About the only way to misplay this shot, and it's a fairly common

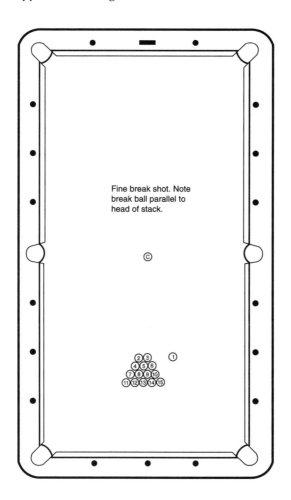

Diagram 34

Fine break shot. Note break ball parallel to head of stack.

error, is to play it with follow and excess speed, trying to get the entire rack open at once. It can be done, but you'll need Dame Fortune perched on your shoulder, and I wouldn't count on her sticking around very long if I were you.

There's also the possibility that the cue ball will sit on that head ball like a lox, the product of a half-hearted attempt at draw. While I surely don't counsel you to use more speed than you can control, all break shots must be struck with authority.

Actually, it's generally a good idea to avoid break shots in which the cue ball must follow after the broken balls; to be reasonably sure of success, you usually need to produce a stroke that sends the cue ball all the way *through* the stack to freedom on the other side. Steve Mizerak, a star in the great Miller Lite commercials of the late '70s and early '80s and the last dominant straight-pool player, will consider follow on a break shot only when the object ball and rack are at least eight inches apart.

That last theory does have some opposition. Consider the same shot, except with the cue ball beginning farther right in the diagram. Now you're cutting the object ball at a considerably sharper angle than before, so your cue ball is traveling more directly into the stack. There is a school of straight-pool thought that believes any time the cue ball is nearer the side rail than the object ball in shots of this nature, the shooter has a clear mandate to use follow on the cue ball, as the opportunity does exist to give the stack a pretty fair pop with minimal risk of a scratch. Personally, I've learned not to make a hard-and-fast rule concerning this decision, even though it's certainly an important decision to make. What I try to do first is apply the rule of tangents to determine which choice of cue-ball hit has the best chance of delivering the cue ball to a corner ball in the stack.

All we've done in Diagram 35 is move the open object ball downtable a ball's width or two—but that's enough to make it a considerably different shot from Diagram 34. It would take the very firmest of draw strokes (and with inside, or left-hand, English at that) to bring the cue ball back to where it at least partially contacts the head ball; compounding the problem, the corner ball cannot be contacted cleanly either, and striking that ball immediately after touching the ball just above it frequently results in a scratch in the near corner pocket. No, this shot just about insists that you take on those dreaded interior balls, and that means it will need a pretty fair clout. Ideally, your draw on the cue ball will be sufficient to pull it to the near side rail and out again; but this shot will often produce less-than-ideal results. There's no way to be certain of cue-ball travel after contact, and while this may seem strange to read, you can't even predict which way the cue ball will be spinning after it meets the stack (that's a result of which clustered balls

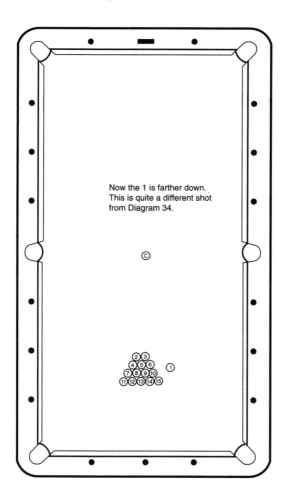

Diagram 35

Now the 1 is farther down. This is quite a different shot from Diagram 34.

it contacts in which order). Not totally infeasible, as I say, but the shot does have certain added challenges.

Move that open object ball still farther downtable where it can meet the corner ball in the rack cleanly, as in Diagram 36, and you have yet another favorable break proposition, much better than that of Diagram 35 but not quite as ideal as Diagram 34. You have some options here, depending on how full or thin you expect to clip that corner ball, one more instance of your rule of tangents rushing to your aid. As you're striking the rack from the side, it will not be possible to draw the cue ball directly back to center table; drawing the cue ball here

Diagram 36

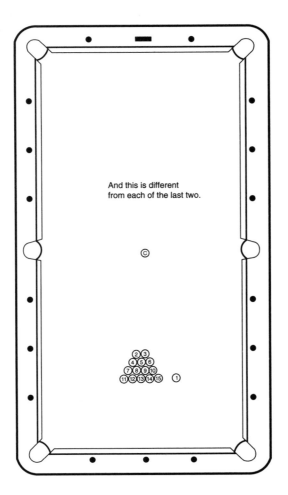

should retard its travel to just a few inches in the direction of the bottom rail. Your next shot will almost surely be one of the interior balls in the back row of the rack.

Follow on the cue ball is, in this instance, not nearly as reprehensible a choice as suggested a few paragraphs earlier. Why do I so readily contradict myself? Because here the cue ball is not following after the object balls; it's following in a counter direction, and should enjoy a safe and happy trip. Some players will even favor modest English, one cue tip northwest of the cue ball's center in the shot diagrammed, to enhance the direction the cue ball is already taking and help it move at

Diagram 37

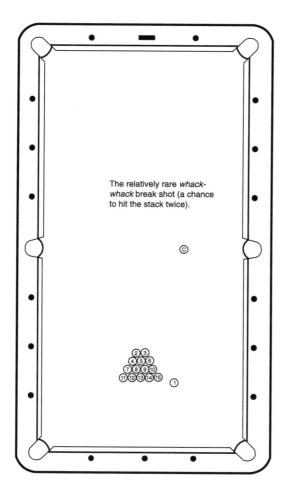

The relatively rare *whack-whack* break shot (a chance to hit the stack twice).

a sharper angle toward center table instead of drifting too far back up the table.

And if the open object ball lies somewhere that the cue ball won't absorb much of that corner ball at all, you have what I somewhat lewdly refer to as a *whack-whack shot* (see Diagram 37). The cue ball actually pops the racked balls twice here. The first contact, as the cue ball travels toward the bottom rail, loosens the balls, then the cue ball comes back off that bottom rail and clobbers them again. Since object-ball travel in this instance is chaotic and totally unpredictable, you will need a measure of luck to succeed with it—but not much, because the

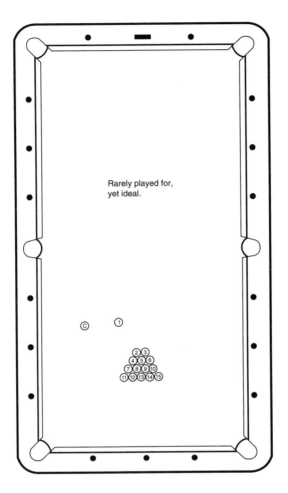

Diagram 38

Rarely played for, yet ideal.

whack-whack shot, properly executed, has as good a chance of open-ing all the balls completely as any other break shot I can think of. The only catch is that such opportunities are fairly rare; further, balls that lie so as to tempt you to try this shot can present the possibility of your missing the stack completely with the cue ball, so be sure to assess the shot carefully. When you get a shot like this, hit the cue ball in its exact center and hard. (If you draw it, it won't come off the bottom rail as fast as you'd like.)

The side-pocket break shot you see in Diagram 38 is frequently overlooked; good straight-pool players usually begin looking for break-shot opportunities into one corner pocket or the other first and fore-

Diagram 39

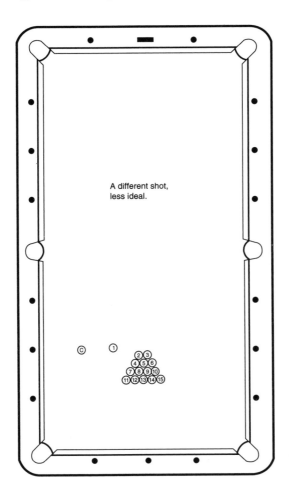

A different shot, less ideal.

most. That's their loss. As long as the shot lies so your cue ball can engage the balls at the top of the stack, this meets every requirement of a good break. You don't have to worry about accessing center table after contact; you're practically there already. And you even enjoy a bigger target, because side pockets are always wider than the corners. Again, cueing the ball below center is advised; you want to retard the cue ball's progress after it separates the cluster, so you're not too far away from your next shot.

Now if both cue ball and object ball were "lower" than presented in Diagram 38—that is, the shot is available to the same side pocket, but your cue ball must now take on the middle balls in the row facing you in the rack as in Diagram 39—you'd have a thorny problem. I wouldn't necessarily advise you to pass up a chance like this altogether, but you should be aware that there are considerable risks. Draw your cue ball on a shot like this, and you unfortunately create excellent prospects for a scratch in the nearest corner. Hit the ball with follow, and you court the agony of your cue ball's being buried in the partially separated balls, leaving you not only shotless but pretty much without a way to play defense either. In short, when you play a side-pocket break shot, you either contact the rack at its thinnest point or else you're depending almost entirely on luck to fetch you a makable next shot.

One other aspect to shots such as this, whether you're using them to open the stack or not: if the intended pocket is not within your field of vision as you sight back and forth from cue ball to object ball, a subtle aiming shift is definitely recommended. Allow your eyes to alternate between object ball and *pocket*, as well as between object ball and cue ball. The rhythm of this will feel a bit different at first, but you should be able to integrate the technique into your game quickly, and it should definitely pay off.

Diagram 40 shows you another form of side-pocket break, a deceptive one this time because while pocketing the object ball alone is quite simple, everything else you want the shot to accomplish is not. You almost *must* contact the top balls in the stack with this one; running into the side of the stack instead presents far too much risk of a scratch. And the cue-ball route from the first ball pocketed to the top of the stack will be trickier to achieve than it looks. Many less-experienced players don't swing the cue ball far enough over to reach those top two balls, not even when they hit the hell out of the shot using draw. Good tip to help "bend" the cue ball's path even more: use reverse draw (left-hand in the diagram).

The break shot of Diagram 41 is another one to avoid, but again, it seems attractive to neophyte players because the object ball is so easy to sink. And again, the problem with it is that it's tricky to engage the stack at a desirable point, complicated further this time by your involving a rail in the shot. You simply *have* to strike the corner ball in

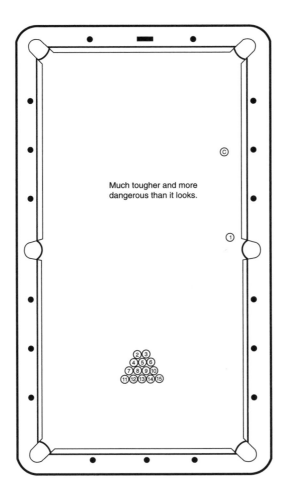

Diagram 40

the rack at least partially here to have any reasonable chance of your cue ball's proceeding to center table, out of trouble. That is not an easy billiard to achieve. If you strike the back row of balls near its middle, once again you're in severe peril of either a scratch or getting stuck there—and it's a lot easier than it looks to miss the stack completely with this shot, often resulting in a scratch into the far corner pocket at the head of the table. When this shot must be played, remember to hit the cue ball low for maximum impact on the stack.

Once you've glanced at Diagram 42, please allow me to advise you to avoid it as you would a spitting cobra unless there are absolutely,

Diagram 41

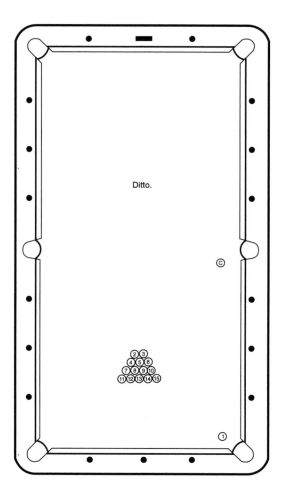

Ditto.

positively no other options. The rail is going to absorb some of your cue ball's speed (unless you overhit it, as if the shot weren't perilous enough already). Thus it becomes more important than ever to contact the stack at a desirable point—which will be extremely difficult here, because you have your hands full just cutting the object ball thin enough, let alone controlling the cue ball's direction accurately after contact. And even if you do manage to send the cue ball into a corner ball in the stack, you have next to no idea where it, or any object balls, are going from there; thus you're trusting luck just about completely. Quite a few players end up with a shot like this as a secondary break shot, after the 14-ball rack has already been broken; it's not a good idea

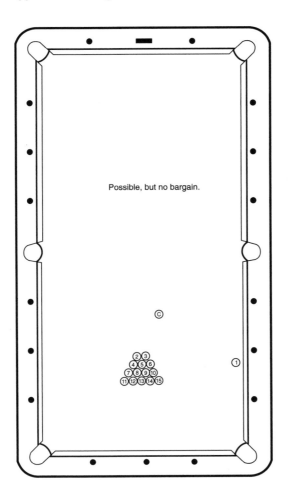

Diagram 42

then either, and usually comes up as the result of an improperly played sequence. There's also a version of this shot from behind the stack, similarly to be shunned with this exception: it's not too bad a secondary break shot provided that (a) there's another object ball on or near the same rail to act as an insurance shot if your cue ball successfully comes off the bottom row of balls, and (b) you don't overhit it, as your angle to the corner pocket is narrow, and hitting such a shot too hard runs the risk of "jawing" the ball.

Last, let's consider two basic forms of the from-the-rear break shots we discussed before, in demonstrating how the table might typically be run. The first things I want you to notice about Diagrams 43 and 44

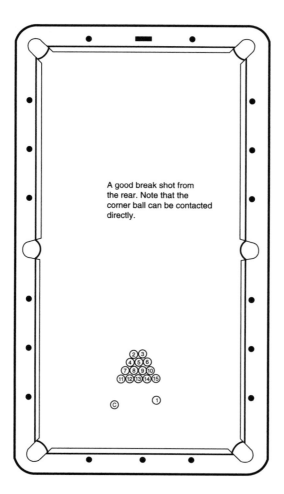

Diagram 43

A good break shot from the rear. Note that the corner ball can be contacted directly.

are the distinctions between the two shots. In Diagram 43, the shot offers you a chance to take on the corner ball cleanly after object-ball contact, plus a favorable angle into that corner ball that greatly increases your chances of sending the cue ball toward center table after it reaches the side rail. In the next diagram, though, your cue ball will not reach the corner ball (not cleanly, anyway), and your angle of approach to it is much flatter anyway.

As you might suppose, those two shots, which are more different than they might appear, are correctly played quite differently. In the version in Diagram 43, which is considerably preferable to the shot of

Diagram 44

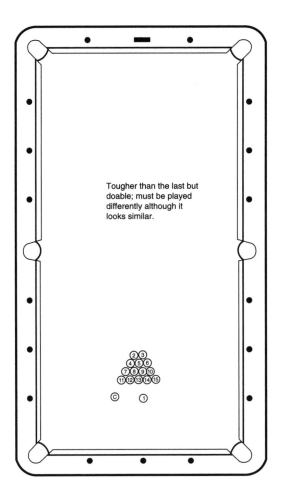

Tougher than the last but
doable; must be played
differently although it
looks similar.

Diagram 44, a tip or so of high outside (left-hand) English and a firm (but not killer-force) stroke should get the cue ball to the rail and thence to center table. The other version of the shot, however, requires you to use the other English (high-right) and send the cue ball off three rails, not one (the side rail ahead of you, then the short rail, then the other side rail) to get decent position for your next shot. Your compensation for the second shot's being more complex: it's nearly impossible to get the cue ball in trouble here if you execute correctly.

And those, believe it or not, are pretty much all the major break shots of straight pool. Naturally, all forms occur on both sides of the table, and with near-limitless variations on precise cue ball/object ball placement and angle to one another, angle of entry into the stack, and so forth. In keeping with that, your straight-pool practice should eventually include acquainting yourself with the possible consequences of all these shots in various attitudes. No two breaks will be identical, of course, which is part of what makes the game so infinite and fascinating; but with experience, you'll develop a feel for which shots yield the best results for the way you hit the ball.

The consensus among straight-pool experts seems to be that break shots that approach the stack from the side are generally best. We've already taken a look at the pros and cons of breaking from behind the stack. The drawbacks, and they're minor ones, to breaking from above the stack—that is, from center table, into one or both of the head balls—are that, since follow must often be used on such a shot, there's a slight chance those first two balls will part and your cue ball will get stuck in the massed balls behind them; or, you might contact one of those head balls right on its schnozzola and separate only the corner ball in its row, even with sufficient cue-ball speed.

Separating clustered balls under control is really the one aspect that separates straight pool from all the other pool games. It's also probably the most difficult facet of cue-ball control, because you're taking on so many obstacles at the same time. You simply *have* to learn to break the balls.

Defense

When a table layout leaves you shotless, it shouldn't be too difficult to leave your opponent shotless from there. If there are no shots anyplace, all you really have to do is leave the landscape as unaltered as possible. If there are shots in a confined area of the table that depend entirely on cue-ball location, all you have to do is keep the cue ball hidden from those shots. But the catch is, neither of those tactics amounts to optimal pool defense.

Say, for instance, that you pocket the open ball that remained for the reracking of the balls, but for whatever reason the cue ball doesn't contact the racked balls (Diagram 45). Suppose further that you and your opponent are equally skilled at barely skimming an object ball (cutting it just as thin as it can be cut without missing it entirely). In theory, you and your opponent could then trade safeties—defensive shots—until the Apocalypse, with your game totally stalemated until and unless one of you leaves something more fertile at which to shoot. That won't happen, of course, but you get the idea.

And that's exactly the point about defensive play in straight pool— any form of the game, really—that eludes a lot of beginners: *the correct objective of a safety is not merely to leave your opponent shotless, but to make it just as thorny as possible for him to leave you shotless.* This gets back to the game-playing skills we alluded to earlier, as well as your ability at pool.

In all forms of the game, a legal requirement for safeties, and in fact for all shots, is that either the cue ball or an object ball must be driven to a rail (or the object ball into a pocket) after cue ball/object ball contact. With that as a given, your first considerations for effective safety play are at opposite ends of the poles, so to speak: either leave the cue ball as far from the object balls as you possibly can, especially on a rail; or leave it just as close to the object balls as possible, which means actually touching or right up against one so that it can't be pocketed and no other ball can be contacted. In the previous example, for instance, a much better response than merely thinning the stack would be to roll the cue ball into the ball just above the corner ball in the stack (Diagram 46), with just enough speed to bunt one object ball to a rail (and two object balls, one to the bottom rail and one to the side, would be even better). Now your opponent is not only shotless, but he has to be very careful about where to send the cue ball so you can't get at the newly open shots. The same sort of smart play is available from above the rack, sticking the cue ball on one of the top two object balls (Diagrams 47 and 48), but it's harder to execute; the head ball must be contacted exactly at the point where it's in line with the three balls in its row.

If those tactics are unavailable to you because of the cue ball's starting position, then the least you'd be striving for would be to leave

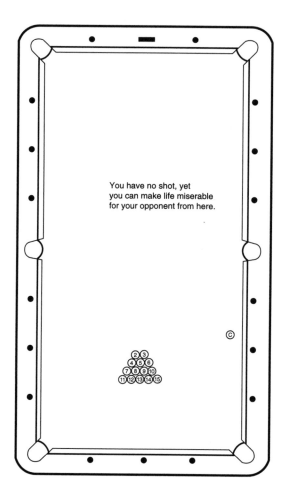

Diagram 45

You have no shot, yet
you can make life miserable
for your opponent from here.

the cue ball on or very near the far end rail. Distance is a potential great equalizer in every form of the game, especially under pressure, and it will not be an easy matter for him to leave you shotless when he has to negotiate a closed stack from far away. (A savvy opponent wouldn't even try; he would most likely roll the cue ball softly off the bottom rail and into the stack for an intentional scratch. We're coming to those.)

Clearly, we cannot diagram every table layout that presents no open shots; we can't even scratch the surface. But the concept of reducing your opponent's defensive options while exercising your own—what

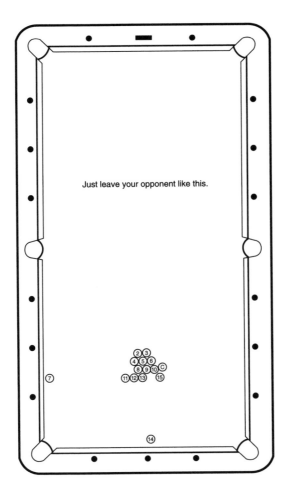

Diagram 46

Just leave your opponent like this.

players call *aggressive defense*—always applies. There are three broad general areas of such defensive opportunities.

Distance

Two subcategories here: leave your opponent far away from the closed rack, or from open but unpocketable balls; or, leave him far away with one open but very dangerous shot to tempt him. The latter situation is commonly known as a *blood test* in pool; it is very difficult to counter except by meeting the challenge of the open ball, and is quite demor-

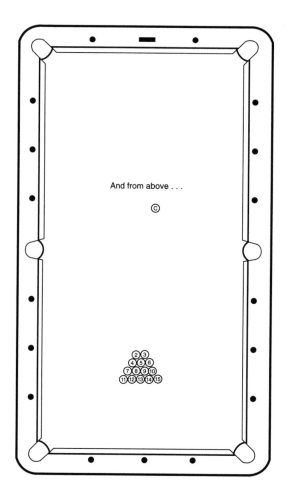

Diagram 47

alizing to your opponent, the value of which is not to be underesti-
mated. (Contrariwise, it's very demoralizing to the defensive player
when his opponent successfully plays through the blood test left for
him. Always strive to be the demoralizer, rather than the demoralizee,
no matter what the scenario. All too true in life as well as in pool.)

The Stack

The opposite of distance, obviously, but still your great and good friend
when it comes to aggressive defense. In a closed stack, the ball next to

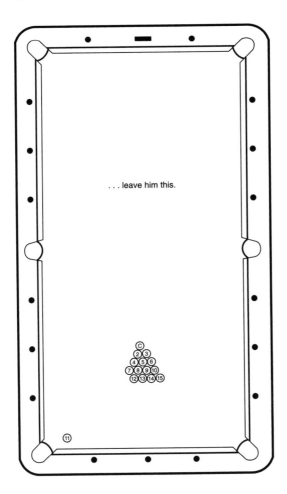

Diagram 48

. . . leave him this.

the corner ball is the only really reliable ball to contact with the cue ball (and that is true from behind the stack, as well as from the side). A point of caution: do *not* attempt the stack-safety of Diagram 46 unless you are reasonably close to the stack to begin with, *and* the cue ball lies on or very close to a line drawn between the ball next to the corner ball in the side row and the ball next to the corner ball in the back row.

Once the stack has been altered, however, and a more or less shapeless cluster remains, you must learn to read that cluster for balls that link up directly to grant you that sort of defensive play. Each cluster of, say, seven or more balls will offer you points that are safe and efficient to contact, and points that carry the worst sort of risk.

Hooks

Also called *snookers*, from the game of that name, hooks are related to defensive plays that utilize the stack; the difference is that this is a possibility when balls are open. A hook permits the incoming shooter a clear view of an object ball, with this critical catch: the accessible ball has no ready path to a pocket, and it blocks your opponent from other object balls that do. In 8-ball, that would mean leaving the cue ball where the only balls immediately available to your opponent are your solids instead of his stripes, or vice-versa; in 9-ball, you'd leave him a clear shot at, say, the 5-ball, except that the ball he needs to contact first is the 3, and the 5 hides him from that. But in straight pool, with all balls theoretically available at all times, it simply means leaving your opponent with a combination shot that has sufficient distance between the object balls to make the shot so low-probability as to be worthless (and multiple object balls are even better; in that case, you don't even need to add maximum distance). The object ball you contact first, in executing this sort of safety, will almost certainly be close to a rail; you simply duck in behind it (see Diagram 49).

The hook is one mighty weapon in 8-ball and 9-ball, games in which only a select number of balls (and just one in 9-ball) are legal targets for your opponent. It's somewhat less efficient in straight pool, because your opponent can easily return the near-identical layout to you just by bunting the nearest ball (unless either that ball or the cue ball becomes frozen to the cushion, in which case one or the other must be driven to another rail for a legal safety).

A related but advanced application of the hook defensive play, especially when your opponent has used an unmakable object ball to hide you from the table's one open shot (assuming that ball is not too near a pocket): use the ball that hooks you to ruin the remaining shot, by either leaving it in front or driving it someplace between the open object ball and its logical pocket. It takes quite a good touch and sense of speed to bring this tactic off, and, of course, you strive for cue-ball distance at the same time. On the positive side, your target area into which to send the first object ball so it spoils the open shot is very

Diagram 49

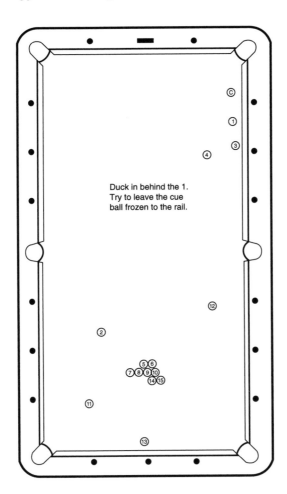

Duck in behind the 1.
Try to leave the cue
ball frozen to the rail.

nearly seven inches wide (almost three ball's widths); and should you succeed in leaving your opponent with distance too, he will have no picnic responding to your shot safely. (See Diagram 50.)

When a table layout denies you any low-risk aggressive defensive opportunities—for example, if you didn't have ready access to the ball next to the corner ball in a closed rack, as discussed above—then the very least you should strive for in your defensive tactics is to leave your opponent as much distance as possible between the cue ball and any hittable object ball.

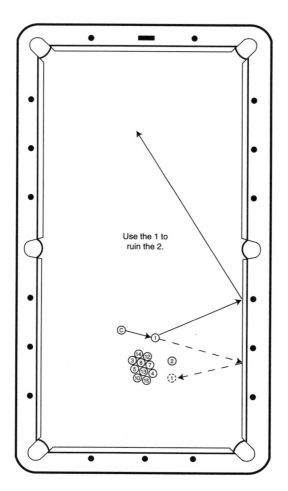

Diagram 50

Use the 1 to
ruin the 2.

Those are actually the basic forms of all pool defense, but their
applications are every bit as infinite as the concepts of position play;
except for your closed-rack opportunities, defensive layouts rarely replicate themselves. If you have the patience for it (and I frankly have
severe problems in this area myself), you might practice playing yourself safe for a few minutes as Irving Crane used to, seeing how many
times in a row you can leave yourself not only shotless but hard-pressed
not to yield an open shot in response.

Any knowledgeable pool player will confirm for you that the ability to leave your opponent without a shot is every bit as important as

the ability to make one yourself, no matter what your game of choice. I will stipulate fearlessly here and now that you will never achieve a level where you sink every single ball you shoot at; no one ever has. Now's the time for you to acknowledge that too, and get into the healthy habit of recognizing table situations that call for defensive thinking—especially those that force you to choose between defensive and offensive options, as well as when the former makes more sense (which will be most of the time, unless you become so conservative that you actually pass up good, fertile offensive opportunities)—and a confident, sensible way to accomplish your defensive plan. Pool defense isn't nearly as much fun to execute as shotmaking. But, as has been said often enough, discretion is the better part of valor. If you become good at defensive play, you'll have something to shoot at in just another inning or two—and besides, good defense wins games. If your mindset is anything like mine, that's where the real fun is.

Straight-Pool Generalities

1. After eyesight, it may well be the second prerequisite of all pool. It's the first element to show up when you're playing well, and among the first to desert you when you're not. (It's also a good thing to watch for—or watch for the absence of—when you're making side bets on somebody else's match.) And for all that significance, it doesn't even have a legitimate vowel to its name. The subject is *rhythm*, friends, and nowhere is it more important than in straight pool, because that particular form of the game has the capacity to keep you at the table for the longest stretches by far.

Your playing rhythm actually begins with the way you assume your stance—another good argument for doing it the same way every single time. Beyond that, you want to spend about the same amount of time in your stance on each shot, take approximately the same number of practice strokes each time, and keep your intervals between individual shots as consistent as you can. It's permissible, and maybe even advisable, to take slightly more time for truly critical shots on which the game might pivot, but don't turn them into mini-melodramas either.

2. The optimal cue-ball speed to apply in any given shot is the absolute *minimum* speed that will get the complete job done (that is, pocket the object ball *and* stop the cue ball someplace desirable, and/or take on secondary object-ball clusters as needed and still get away cleanly). Minimal force usually represents maximized cue-ball control. This advice, however, proposes a caveat of common sense: unless you're playing on brand-new equipment that you know to be flawless (and maybe not even then), you're begging for trouble by shooting softly. Most tables in this cosmos have their own idiosyncrasies and rolls, owing to age, climate, wear and tear, and other factors; unless the table in question is really lopsided and its rolls are truly horrible, the way you overcome a table's playing imperfections is with sufficient cue-ball and object-ball speed.

Do *not*, however, overhit the balls. It's an extremely common beginner's error; almost as often, it's a symptom of anxiety, costs you accuracy, and is near-suicidal on tables with "tough" pockets.

Somewhere between those two extremes is obviously the correct choice. Exactly where? That's for you to determine, from your own sense of speed and playing experience; your basic rule of thumb is to shoot hard enough that the balls roll straight, yet soft enough that you can still develop your sense of speed and touch.

3. I continue to believe that pool imitates life. Your own game, strategically and executionally, ought to have your own personality in it.

4. A great habit to fall into at once: each time you come to the table to shoot, and/or any time the pressures of the game force you to slow down, take a hike around the table and inspect your layout from all vantages before you shoot anything. Not only will this help you beat pressure, it will improve your position concepts without your being aware of giving them any conscious thought.

5. An excellent concept for learning position play: spot the balls nearest the four corner pockets, and try to get them in succession. Some-

times this will create a position pattern in which your cue ball circles the perimeter of the layout; sometimes you'll have the opportunity to cut diagonally across that layout instead or as well. This is where true *pattern* position-play begins.

6. Another fairly advanced principle of position play: the skilled application of inside English—that is, English on the same side of the cue ball as the direction of your cut shot—will improve your position play enormously, for a variety of reasons. It may take some getting used to, but get comfortable with this option, even on thin cut shots.

Here's an idea of the potential advantages of the technique:

- It can be a great inhibitor of cue-ball speed coming off rails (when it acts as *reverse* English; it doesn't always).

- Similarly, it can minimize the angle at which your cue ball deflects off the rail.

- On shots that are not quite straight-in, inside draw can help you bring the cue ball back near its point of origin. (Neither center nor outside draw can help you accomplish anything of the kind.)

- Regarding the rule of tangents we considered earlier, while draw in general will create an angle of deflection in excess of 90 degrees, crisp inside draw will create the widest angles of all.

- On cut shots, inside English permits you to hit the object ball a tad thinner, altering your cue ball's path accordingly, should your table layout make that desirable.

- Inside English does a lot to neutralize the dreaded cling factor discussed earlier; thus you're better able to aim the shot as it actually lies.

- Perhaps best of all, it offers a focus for your position planning. Competitive pressure often causes players, even very good ones, to encounter all kinds of mental interference even as they contemplate open shots. *What's available here that inside English will help me do?* is not a bad secondary question at all to ask yourself (after such logical queries as *What can I make here without disturbing anything else? What can I make without using any English or rails? What's my plan for dealing with the trouble shots?*, and so on).

Because inside English is really more of an advanced-play tool, we'll limit our examination of it to the above playing edges. But keep in mind that your comfortably adding it to your game will, by itself, place you well above your peers.

7. Shut up. Of course pool and camaraderie go hand in hand, but talking to individuals or generally playing to the crowd while still at the table is one of the most certain self-destruction tactics. And it's at its most insidious in straight pool, where you're at the table longer.

8. Some good tension fighters: Put your teeth together, just lightly enough that you can feel them touch. Try to relax the base of your spine and the back of your tongue. Breathe deeply; this is universally recognized as one of the great "stress-busters" in all walks of life.

9. In all forms of pool, try to look as good as you can while at the table (without getting fancy or doing anything else totally unnatural). It's a virtually automatic game-improver. Visualize and execute "the thoroughbred look," and you'll leave opponents in your dust.

10. Similarly, tournament tennis players are taught not to slump their shoulders after losing points; it gives away a psychological edge. Apply this same principle to your pool game, and play emotionlessly. You should see beneficial results almost at once.

11. By all means, rehearse each shot mentally before attempting it; see yourself completing the shot successfully, as basketball players are trained to do with their free throws. And if you picture yourself missing a shot for any reason, get out of your shooting stance and re-prepare yourself mentally. Creating a television screen in your head and watching yourself play on it is potentially even more valuable than videotaping yourself.

12. Don't settle for merely breaking clusters open. Look for the cue-ball point of contact with the cluster, and try to have some idea of how far you intend to move the separated balls, as well as what the cue ball is going to do after contact with the cluster.

13. Every time a cluster has been altered in the slightest way, examine it carefully before shooting. It doesn't take much to turn a ball that can't possibly be made into one that can't possibly be missed.

14. Train yourself to *observe* the results of your game, rather than falling into the treacherous trap of *judging* them. A super lesson for life as well as pool.

15. A good slump-buster: change your playing pace *radically*. (Once you've hit your stride again, you'll settle naturally into a more familiar and comfortable rhythm.)

16. In straight pool, and in fact all of the game's other forms too, it may well benefit you to stop thinking in terms of "shooting pool" or "pocketing balls," and more in terms of playing a game. Yes, shooting balls into holes is where most of the fun is in pool. But I think you'll be far better at that, and thus have far more fun, if you begin to regard poolplaying in general, and shotmaking in particular, as a matter of moving a piece—the cue ball—all over a game board. That's what the game is really about.

Why all this detailing of a pool game that fewer and fewer players favor? Because it's by far the best possible foundation to lay for learning the game that everybody plays, 8-ball—and that chapter is next. Hopefully you'll have given these straight-pool concepts enough thought that they'll be recognizable right away as we examine 8-ball. Before we move on to that, though, let's analyze the successful running of one more straight-pool rack, according to the principles we've considered. In fact, let's analyze it as run two separate ways, and see if we can determine which (if either) is the better solution and why (Diagrams 51 through 78).

Just in case you're curious as to how I worked through this, I first ran the rack diagramming my shot sequence one ball at a time, then went back and recreated the break-shot crossroads I faced after my first three open shots, per my diagram of it. While I'll concede this methodology is probably not absolutely accurate, it's close enough for our purposes that we can learn from the differences in the two position executions.

If Diagram 51 looks familiar to you, you're my kind of student; it replicates Diagram 30. As previously stated, it's a typical enough leave, and besides it lets us examine either of two possible secondary break shots, the 10 or 1. (Back in Diagram 30, you'll recall we took a look at the results of playing the 1 secondarily rather than immediately; we'll examine that route again, as an example of the game's infinite flexibility. But bear with me; there are good lessons in the following sequences too.) So we play the 3 with enough high-center English on the cue ball to take advantage of the window between the 9 and 10 (Diagram 52). In order to use the 10 to go to work on the still-massed balls, we only need roll the 8 in softly, with minimal cue-ball travel after contact (Diagram 53). Even though we achieve decent break-shot position on the 10, we want to play it under control, to be sure of having at least the 9 as a next-shot option. (Too many players would go all-out on the 10, hoping to separate most or all of the stacked balls and willing to take potluck on where all those balls roll, including the cue ball. That *might* work, but I prefer certainties to probabilities, and you will, too.) Keep this point of the rack in mind; we'll be coming back to it shortly, when we take a look at running the rack by breaking from the front instead of the rear. (That distinction begins with the concept of getting on the right side of the ball, already discussed.)

Diagram 54 shows you a perfectly acceptable set of results. Some of the remaining balls still need to be separated, but there are open shots in addition to the 9 we saved, and a workable plan is beginning to form. The only remaining object balls that must be moved somehow, even if minimally, are the 5 and 1, and the 12 and 13. I could get at the 5-1 tandem right now by shooting the 14, but the reason I'd think

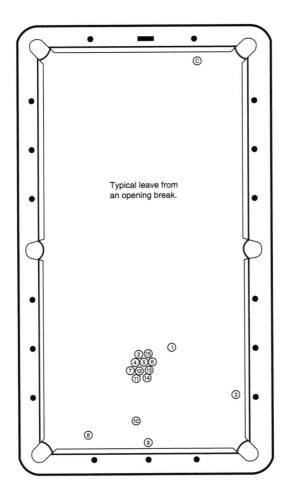

Diagram 51

Typical leave from an opening break.

twice about that is there's no ready safety valve for it. If the 6, for instance, were very close to the side pocket, then I'd be set; but as it is, I can't predict exactly what the cue ball will do after meeting the 5, and *there's no point in gambling when sure things exist*.

The professional way to solve this layout is with an "around the horn" approach, making the 6 in the far corner, the 15 in the opposite side, and the 7 in the near corner, all with minimal cue-ball travel after contact and without disturbing anything (Diagrams 55 through 57). Now, in Diagram 57, I have a good angle on the 11 to move the 12 and

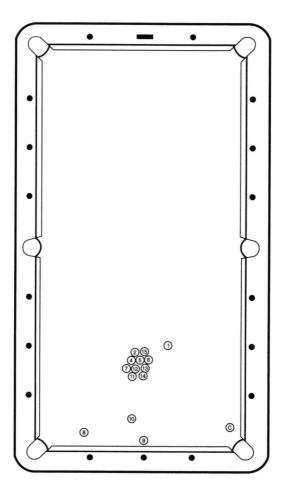

Diagram 52

13. Depending on the precise angle of deflection those balls take, I might get a bonus and separate the 5-1 as well, but what I'll be sure to do is get the cue ball clear of the 12 after contact so I have at least some next-shot options.

Also, it's not too early at this point to begin thinking about what the break shot for my next frame will be. If I could move either the 1 or 5 without disturbing the other ball much, one of those would be fine; but the 4 is ideal just as it lies right now, with the 2 in good position to lead me right to it. So I'll count on those.

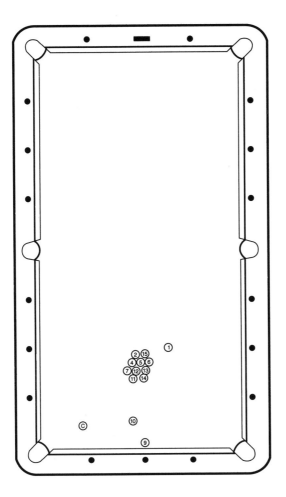

Diagram 53

As you can see in Diagram 58, the results of my 11-ball break shot have left the 13 somewhere advantageous to separating the 1 and 5. But even if I hadn't caught that good break by sending the cue ball toward center table, I maximized my chances of having *something* productive to do next. In Diagram 59, the 13 is gone and all problems have been solved; now (and, ideally, *only* now) is the time for a shot sequence that includes the 9 that has been waiting so patiently as a full-time safety valve on the bottom rail. Diagrams 60 through 65 show you how I went: 12-9-14-1(in a far corner; don't forget to inspect your layout

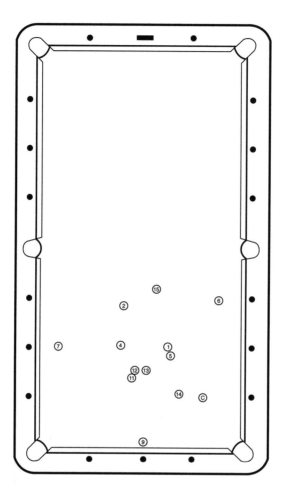

Diagram 54

from all directions)-5-2, leaving the 4 and the cue ball right where I want them. It might sound a tad wordy in the analyzing, but that rack was really quite easy to run.

Now let's revisit Diagram 51 briefly. Having already decided that I'd rather not use the 10 to rebreak the stacked balls, I would try for a slightly different angle on the 8 in pocketing the 3. It's a subtle distinction, no doubt about that, but this is a game of subtleties. By sending the cue ball as little as a half-ball's width either beyond or short of where I did before, I have an angle on the 8 that will enable me to get

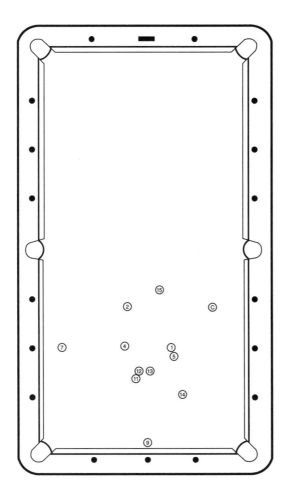

Diagram 55

a *non*breaking angle on the 10. Diagram 66 shows you about where I'd like to be on the 8, so I can execute the two-rail position ploy of Diagram 28 (go on back and check it out; I'll wait here) and get to center table for the 1 (Diagram 67).

In Diagram 68, note that although I've made favorable progress by breaking with the 1, four balls of that original cluster have not moved in the least. That's not uncommon at all, and it's a good example of why your break-shot plan should always include an avenue of escape for your cue ball. You simply cannot count on separating every single ball

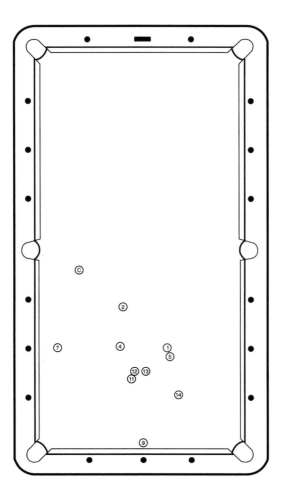

Diagram 56

with a break shot. But I have a good chance to deal with the remaining cluster by shooting the 6 with just enough draw for an angle on the 13 (Diagram 69).

Diagram 70 shows you the results of breaking with the 13: all problems solved, with a logical next-frame break shot (the 11) and a logical key ball (the 4) to get me to that break shot. All the remaining balls can be picked off cleanly without moving anything if the cue ball is correctly managed, and I chose a crisscross-type pattern of 15-2-5-7-12-14-9-4 (Diagrams 71 through 78).

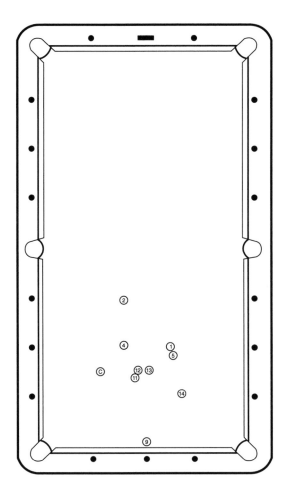

Diagram 57

Now, was either of those two run-the-table executions preferable to the other for some reason? Well, certainly not when it comes to the score; and beyond that, we can't reasonably draw any lasting conclusions from just one example. But my opinion is that most professional players would have opted for the second approach, even though the 1 has no immediate safety valve, while the 10 did. The pros choosing this concept of position play would most likely reason that it's the easiest way to keep the cue ball in the middle of the table, and besides there are just too many risks involved with attacking the rack at its broadest

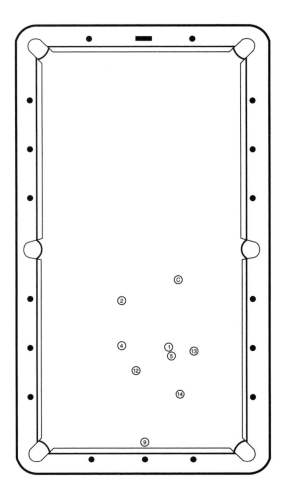

Diagram 58

point instead of its narrowest. The game's experts rate break shots from the side, or even front, well ahead of those from the rear.

Here's the argument in favor of the first approach, since it does have its proponents, even though they tend to be the minority: since you began with a secondary break shot that had a safety valve with it, you never have to hit the balls particularly hard. With the 10, and subsequent rebreak shots within the rack, you tend to keep more balls in the vicinity of the rack, where they offer more options for next-frame break shots (we had four, remember). Then why don't more players endorse the from-the-rear straight-pool position concept? Because it's

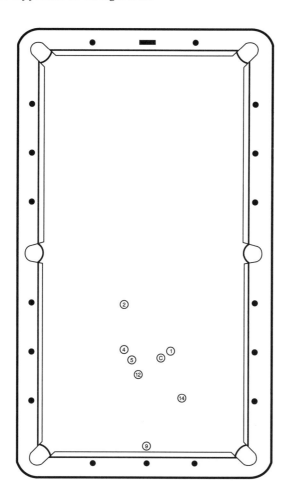

Diagram 59

a finesse approach, developed in the era of clay-composition, not plastic, balls, which makes a humongous difference in itself; and the approach was developed by players who competed at very little *but* straight pool, and those players seem to be going the way of the passenger pigeon. Virtually all of today's top players are shot-drillers who excel at their (and TV's) first choice, 9-ball, totally unaccustomed to "babying" object balls the way yesterday's straight-poolists did.

I'll have to concede that unless you and a pool buddy discover straight pool at the same time, you're probably going to have some trouble finding any competition at it. But I hope you persevere, at least to

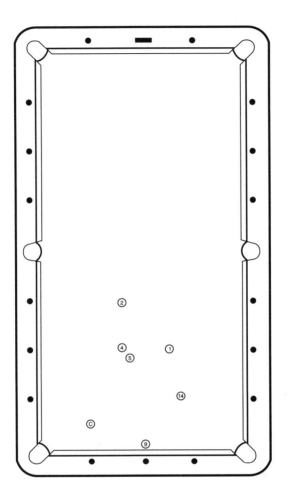

Diagram 60

the point of making the game a staple of your practice. As I've said before, I or any other qualified teacher could make a top straight-pool player out of a top 9-ball player long, long before we could ever achieve the reverse. But at this stage of your development at pool, there is simply no better teacher of all the pool games than this one. Fall in love with it at once. You won't be sorry.

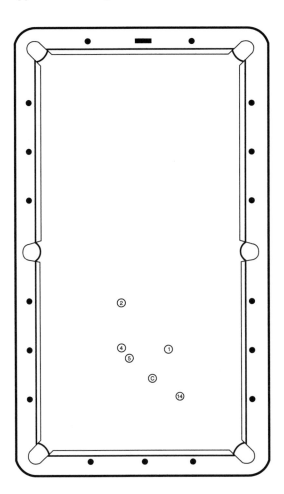

Diagram 61

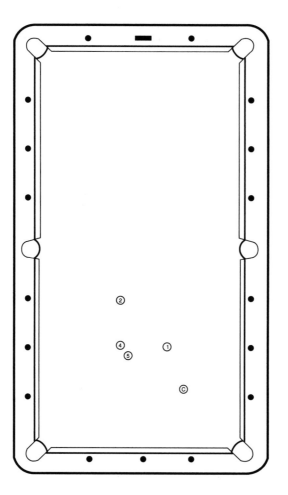

Diagram 62

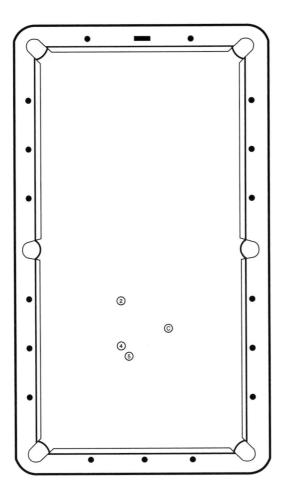

Diagram 63

Diagram 64

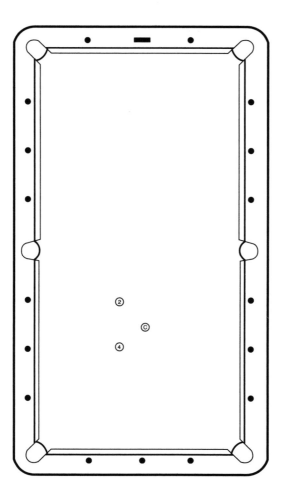

Diagram 65

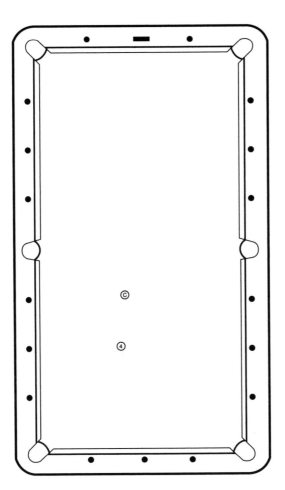

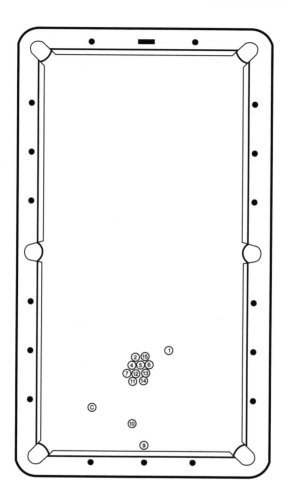

Diagram 66

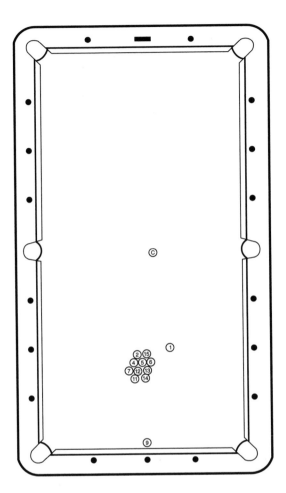

Diagram 67

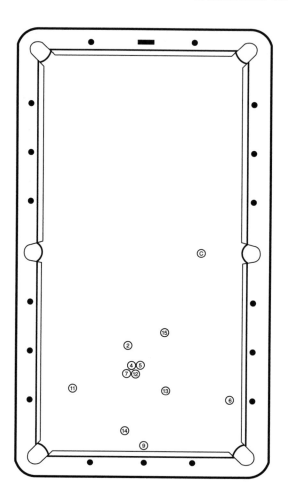

Diagram 68

Diagram 69

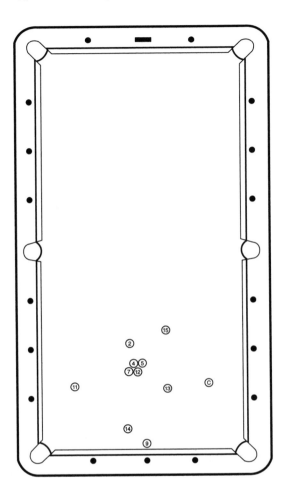

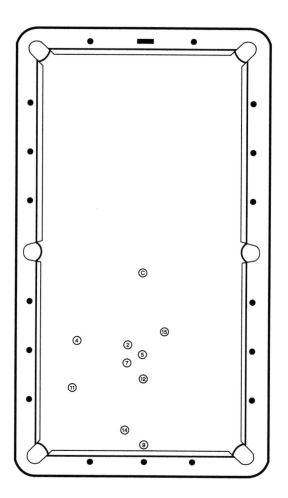

Diagram 70

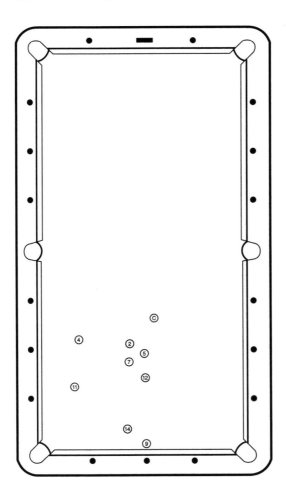

Diagram 71

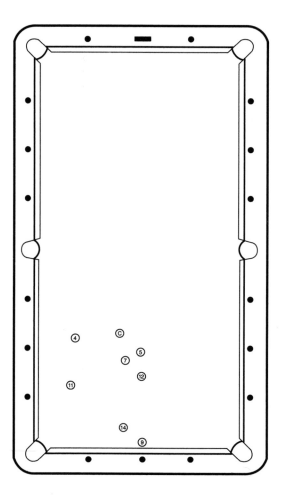

Diagram 72

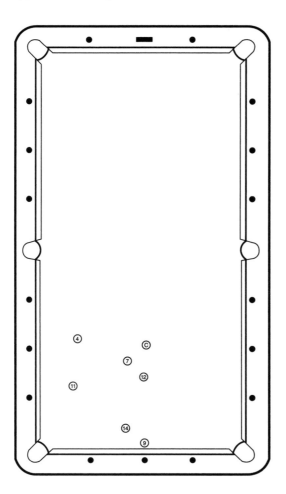

Diagram 73

Diagram 74

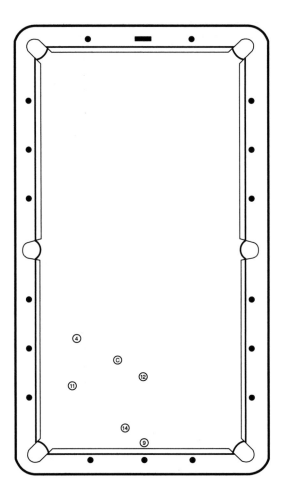

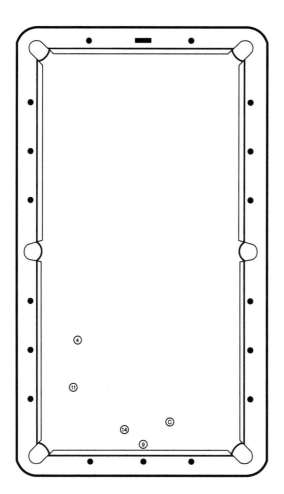

Diagram 75

Diagram 76

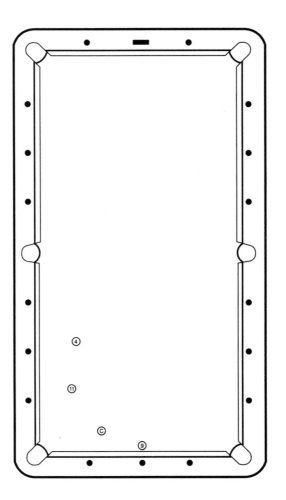

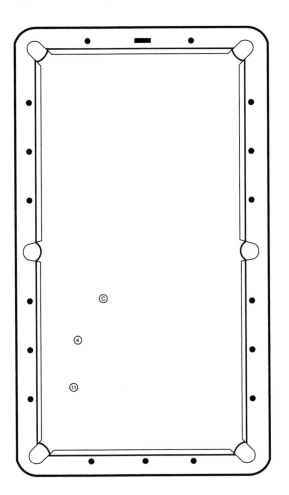

Diagram 77

Diagram 78

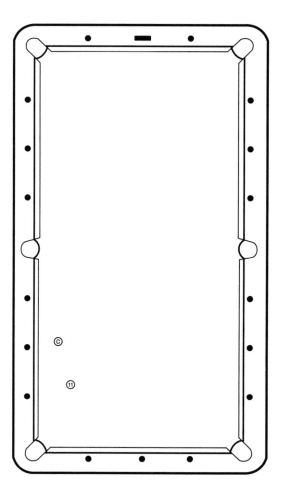

6

A SMARTER APPROACH
TO 8-BALL

This is probably the game that introduced you to pool (even if you did call it "stripes and solids" way back then). It's the game around which entire leagues, comprising hundreds of thousands of players nationally, are organized. Among the vast majority of the 44 million-plus people estimated to play pool at least once annually, 8-ball is unquestionably the game of choice.

And almost everybody plays it incorrectly.

The first 8-ball lesson for you to learn, assuming you have even modest familiarity with the game, is to stop perceiving it as some kind of kid's pastime. Even though you do see it played a lot by kids and beginners, 8-ball is really a subtle, deceptive game that borrows from whatever skills you have from whatever other form of pool you know. And none of those skills count more in 8-ball than straight-pool skills. If two good 8-ball players go head-to-head, in the long run the better straight-pool player between them should win.

In fact, there are really only two major distinctions. First, in 8-ball, you blast the balls open to begin the game. That alone makes it totally unfeasible for me to take you through a typical pattern; there is no such thing. What we can do is see how straight-pool principles apply to any given layout.

Now, despite that blast-break that opens the game, 8-ball is not (or should not be) a game of luck. If you want to begin winning a much higher percentage of the 8-ball games you play, you're going to have to embrace the second distinction between 8-ball and straight pool, and it's an unorthodox one indeed: *in 8-ball, pocketing balls can very easily be to your disadvantage.*

That is not a typographical error. I know you've been focused on getting a ball into a hole ever since, well, you called 8-ball "stripes and solids." After all, that's how you get a second consecutive turn, and after you sink enough balls, you win, right?

Well, yes and no, especially in 8-ball. Sure, if you can pocket your seven striped or solid balls plus the 8 consecutively in a single turn at the table, you win. But 8-ball is simply not going to present you with that many such opportunities—especially not on the smaller-than-regulation-size tables that you'll find in most bars (where the vast majority of all pool, including leagues, is played today), where you have the same number of balls but typically 16 square feet less playing area in which to manage them. Most of the time, you'll be looking at table layouts that offer both open shots and stymies. And the critical point to be made here is this: unless you have a sound plan for dealing with each trouble spot to free your tied-up object balls, you're slitting your own throat by sinking the balls that are already free.

Larry Schwartz, author of an excellent book called *The 8-Ball Handbook for Winners* and a member of a repeating national champion team, states the case in these intriguing terms: "Think of 8-ball as military strategy. Each ball you make, when you *don't* run out the game, represents a dead soldier who can no longer help you win the war."

Less morosely, each ball you sink represents one more ball you cannot use to hide the cue ball behind and play your opponent safe. And 8-ball, correctly played, involves far more safety play than you'd think.

At the same time, when you have fewer balls on the table than your opponent, it becomes far easier for him to play you safe, because he has more places to duck the cue ball. Unless your remaining balls are situated right in front of pockets, it's so much easier for him to avoid those table areas where he'd be leaving *you* with anything good to shoot at.

When you have more balls left than your opponent does, that's very much to your advantage—which is probably just the opposite of what you'd normally think. In fact, if he gets down to his last few balls (the fewer the better) and doesn't win the game outright from there, and you have lots of balls left, you're a solid favorite to win the game as long as you play correctly!

Yet the vast majority of 8-ball players will immediately commence firing at the first open balls they see. Apparently it's too tough a habit to break (or they don't know any better; but now you do)—or deliberately *not* pocketing balls is too tough a nuance to pick up. So there's a whole universe of pool players out there you can beat by playing smarter, even if they are better shotmakers than you. The case can be stated even more unequivocally than that: the only time you should go for a winning runout in 8-ball is when you're absolutely certain that you will run out. (Note that I didn't say *can* but *will*; the difference is critical.) At all other times, concentrate on safe leaves for your opponent. Let him shoot balls into holes, or try to, while you instead play the game as it should be played. It's not unlike a boxer versus a brawler; the boxer should win if he doesn't make any mistakes. It will also be devastating psychologically to your opponent to come to the table repeatedly without open shots, and that's yet another edge for you. (Playing the game defensively like this, by the way, may not make you overwhelmingly popular. But did you come to win or to socialize?)

You must make one solid, or striped, ball as intended (and a brief examination of rules in general follows shortly) in order to commit yourself to that category of balls for the duration of the game. As the game progresses, depending on the specific layout, there may be a benefit to your pocketing a ball or two when you can still leave your opponent completely safe by so doing and/or accomplish an outright win. Otherwise, it will generally be far more worthwhile to leave your balls near pockets, in "will-call" fashion, than in those pockets; and almost as valuable to leave your balls on rails between your opponent's ball(s) and the pockets.

Further, the only proper times to separate the clusters that have your balls tied up are when you have both an open shot that will send your cue ball into the cluster *and* a safety-valve ball (see the straight-pool principles emerging here?) that you can count on shooting next no matter where those newly separated balls go. For excellent explanations on 8-ball strategy, I recommend not only Larry Schwartz's book but two fine instructional videos by expert player Jim Reid called *The Art of 8-Ball* and *No Time for Negative*; ask your billiards-supply outlet if they can order those for you.

Now let's take a look at some playing examples, starting with how you select stripes or solids. First, you and your opponent, assuming you do not face each other regularly, should always—*always*—agree on 8-ball's playing rules before you begin. This will help avoid disputes, and maybe even mayhem. Depending on where it's being played, 8-ball has practically infinite sets of rules regarding how the balls should be racked, how one player or the other acquires stripes or solids, what happens if you make the 8 on the break, what happens if you don't contact one of your own balls legally with the cue ball, and so on. Most of the time you'll be playing by whatever rules are commonly played in that particular location, usually known as *house rules*. But assuming you're playing under current Billiard Congress of America rules (and they publish the game's official rule book), the most important of these rules are as follows:

1. The balls can be racked any way you choose, as long as the 8 is in the middle and the two bottom-corner positions in the rack are occupied by one striped ball and one solid, rather than two of either.

2. Sinking the 8 on the break neither wins nor loses the game out-right; it is simply respotted.

3. A player is not committed to either stripes or solids until she sinks a ball *as intended* (that is, balls that go in on the break stay down but don't count toward committing the shooter, even if

more solids fall than stripes or vice versa; the table is still "open" until one player makes a ball in the pocket he meant to).

4. Should a player fail to contact the required striped or solid ball first with the cue ball, once that committment has been made, that player's opponent gets cue ball in hand (that is, the cue ball may be placed anywhere on the table, and any legal ball is fair game).

Breaking the Balls

The 8-ball break looks like a brute-strength, "hit and hope" proposition, but it's not. Actually, it should be a controlled stroke with a definite beginning, middle, and end, just like any other pool stroke. (Which is not to say, by the way, that you should break with your regular ball-pocketing stroke; you should not.) However, you might well consider some adjustments when taking your stance, forming your bridge, and delivering. Most players spread their legs a bit wider on the break, for instance, and lengthen their bridge by a few inches; some also hold the cue a bit lower with their stroking hand. But what's essential is that you don't allow yourself to become excited about hitting the ball with all your might. Instead, maintain the regular rhythm of your practice strokes without rushing into the break itself.

Uncontrolled speed actually does some horrific things to your break. At the very outset of your stroke, your practice strokes lose rhythm because you're dwelling on all that force you're about to summon. Ditto your mental rehearsals; they suffer because instead of seeing and feeling control and smoothness, you're thinking power. The arc in your backswing will be tremendously exaggerated, making it much harder to keep the actual stroke level. You'll be less accurate in hitting the cue ball where you want to—dead center—and at that peak speed, your unwanted, uncontrolled English will be magnified many times after impact. You'll probably also be less accurate about hitting the head ball in the rack where you want to (right on the nose).

That's what you're sacrificing when you just rear back and fire. What you get in return is a *possibility*—no more—that some of the object balls will roll a few inches or maybe feet farther, which is no guarantee that they'll fall someplace as a result. And worst of all, your cue ball is probably flying around like a balloon with its air just released, with up to 15 object balls moving around simultaneously. In short, you have nothing going for you at this point but Dame Fortune to help you sink a ball and get a shot at a second one. Don't trust that fickle lady all that often.

Rhythm and concentration will help you control the speed you need for the break. Hit it hard, sure, but be certain that your stroke has a beginning, middle, and end, and not the brute-strength herky-jerky lunge you see all the time. Tighten your grip on the butt slightly, but no more than that. Then stroke the shot smooth and pure. You'll get maximum impact as well as control if you hit the cue ball dead center; it will arrive at the stack with no natural spin of its own for the balls to absorb; and remember, with that kind of impact, any English at all would be tremendously increased.

If your stroke is level, a center-ball hit on the cue ball that travels into the head ball dead-on from where you begin will produce this effect: the cue ball will be rejected in the direction of center table, and *it should die there*. Don't mistake this for the force-follow effect, in which the cue ball makes contact, backs up, and then plows in again for little second-effort spurts. That happens when you inadvertently hit the cue ball above center; it's very dramatic to see and probably makes you think of spectacular Freudian things too, but it's still uncontrolled and dangerous. The center of the table is where your cue ball will be safest from all those flying missiles, and if you've stroked the break correctly, you're a favorite to make something and have the rest pretty well open. And you can parlay that into a mighty big edge.

Where in the stack should you send the cue ball? That depends on what rules you and your opponent have agreed to. If, for instance, you've agreed to play that you win by sinking the 8 on the break, there

Diagram 79

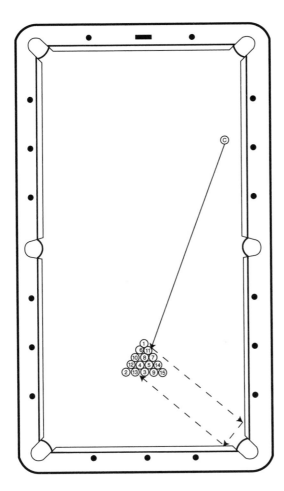

is a breaking technique that could send the 8 in the direction of a side pocket (although, on balance, this remains a very low probability). This break is illustrated in Diagram 79: place your cue ball to the side of the table (but far enough off the rail that you can bridge and stroke comfortably), and aim for the ball just behind the head ball in the rack. Use low inside English—right-hand in the diagram—and you have another form of the naughtily named whack-whack shot, whacking the stack once on the way in and a second time coming off those two bottom rails. In theory, the 8 doesn't go far as a result of your first contact; it just hangs around waiting for the second impact to move it out.

Wherever it goes, this double-whammy approach should do a pretty efficient job of separating the racked balls. You *must* utilize the inside English, otherwise you're unlikely to bend back to that long rail or come off the bottom rail with anywhere near the speed you want.

If, on the other hand, you're playing by the contemporary rule that you *don't* win by sinking the 8 on the break, why break as though you were? What most good players will do when playing 8-ball (or 9-ball, for that matter; the balls are blasted open to begin that game, too) is find the table's "live" areas for breaking, just as bowlers read the grooves and rolls of unfamiliar lanes. (The side of the table, as described in the previous paragraph, is a good starting place; so is the table's head spot, directly opposite that head ball you're preparing to smash.) No matter where you break from, though—unless you're trying the technique of Diagram 79—your objective is to pop that head ball just as fully as you can, keeping your cue level and striking the cue ball in its exact center. The effect you're striving for is for the cue ball to leap back from its initial contact and stop dead in the center of the table. This should give you the maximum number of shooting options.

Don't fall victim to too much body English, even though competitive pressure can make it mighty tough to avoid. All that jumping and twisting around adds nothing whatsoever to your stroke, and could be detrimental if you leap out of your shooting stance too early. Advanced players do have their quirks for achieving added leverage when breaking. Some plant their front legs under the table and actually brace against that contact; others push off their back legs at the moment of cue-ball contact. One rising star, Minnesota's Jimmy Wetch, leans so far over the table in his breaking stance that he resembles the Leaning Tower of Pisa. But be satisfied with a solid stance and executing your stroke with as much cue-ball speed as you can control—no more.

Winning with Offense—or Defense

There wouldn't be much point to overwhelming you with 8-ball's hidden complexities while you're still learning. So let's take a look at a few situations that offer outright-win possibilities, plus a few that do not. Probably the most valuable lesson you can learn when you first come to this game is to distinguish runout opportunities from those where your defensive options are potentially an equally powerful weapon.

Let's say your opponent has broken to begin the game, and nothing has gone in. As you come to the table, with the choice of stripes or solids still available to you, here's what you want to ask yourself:

1. Where are the trouble spots, in the form of clustered balls that must be separated before they become pocketable?

2. Are there any solid balls blocking a stripe's path to a pocket, or vice versa?

3. Are there any balls within, say, two inches of a side pocket, yet too close to the rail to be pocketed easily? (If the answer is yes, either choose the other category of balls or formulate a plan for moving them; that's a stinky place for an object ball, in all forms of pool.)

4. Does any single object ball tie up the 8-ball? (If so, choose that category of balls; sink one and you have a built-in assurance that your opponent can't run out—unless, of course, he comes up with a way to move your ball and/or the 8 himself.)

In Diagram 80, for instance, the balls have really been broken well. There are no clusters; almost equally important, there aren't any balls close enough together, or close to a rail, to offer you any handy weapons for hiding the cue ball from your opponent's stripes or solids once you sink something. It's probably worthwhile to try winning this game from the outset; a logical progression in your position sequence would be to choose stripes and go 9-15-14(those last two into the same side pocket)-10-13-12-11(probably into the opposite side)-8. If you mess up along the way, it wouldn't look particularly good for you, for reasons already discussed plus a layout this open; but there's always the possibility that you'll get lucky on your miss and accidentally leave your opponent in a tough spot or totally shotless, or that he'll mess up

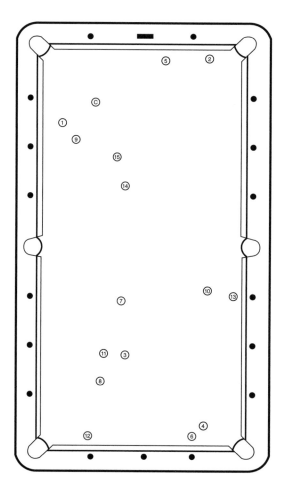

Diagram 80

just as you did. Strategically, though, it does make sense to go for it with a layout offering you so many open shots. Most 8-ball layouts, especially immediately following the break, will combine open shots with trouble spots and/or balls still clustered.

Diagram 81 shows you just such a layout, and the combination of positives and negatives here would make most players stop and think. An accomplished player could win from here with the solids; even though the 3 and 6 are still trapped in a cluster, the 2 offers a natural angle from which to separate that cluster, and the 4 and 1, close nearby, offer good safety-valve shots after the cluster is separated. But that is

Diagram 81

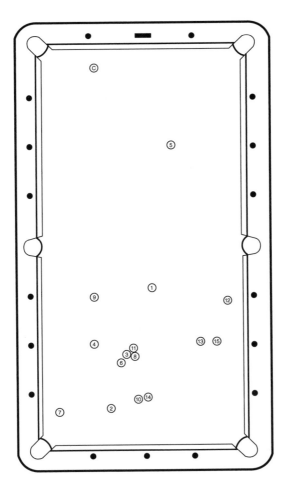

fairly advanced, and if you're not quite ready for intermediate-or-better status, there are excellent defensive possibilities here that prob-ably make more sense for you. Make the 7, committing yourself to solids for the game, then just miss the 2, rolling the cue ball softly up against the 10, shutting off your opponent's direct view of any other striped balls. (See Diagrams 82 and 83. But do remember, in executing this brilliant play, that when you play defense—in fact, on all shots in all forms of pool—either the cue ball or the object ball must touch a rail after cue ball/object ball contact. So don't make the fairly common mistake of playing your safety too softly; otherwise it's a foul and your

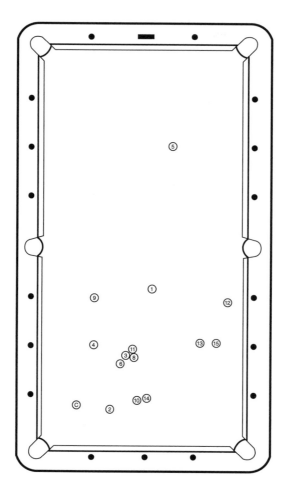

Diagram 82

opponent gets cue ball in hand. Get the 2 to a rail, parking it just out-side the opposite corner pocket.)

Always stay alert for object balls close to a rail like this, especially early in the game. They represent potentially easy and effective defensive moves like the one above.

Not much dilemma in Diagram 84; this one clearly offers very little chance of an outright win, and only the most rank of beginners would approach it that way. So just drive that 5 out of there, and park the cue ball underneath the 6 and 13, as in Diagram 85. (Invoke the rule

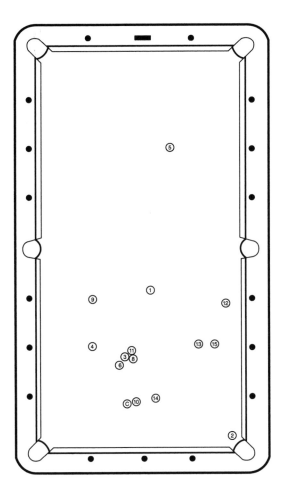

Diagram 83

of tangents in determining exactly where the object ball you contact and the cue ball will be going; it's just as valid on shots where you're *not* trying to sink anything as on those where you are. You can even make it work in reverse, something like this: *If I want the cue ball to go directly from the 5 to beneath the 6 and 13, and I strike the cue ball exactly in its middle, what path for the 5 should I be aiming for to create a 90-degree angle from the path of the cue ball?*) This tactic will leave your opponent nothing; even better, he's probably not used to responding to 8-ball safeties. That means he must take on a whole new

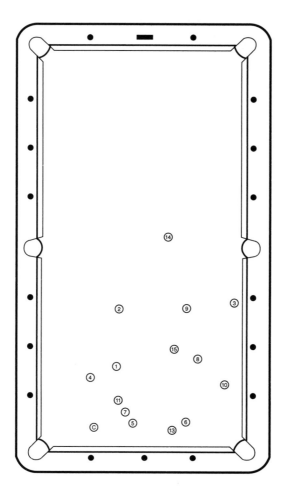

Diagram 84

mind-set for this decidedly mental game, which is no easy psychological task. Each time you leave your opponent shotless, you send him into
a nasty little self-struggle, wondering if he is being outsmarted.

Can you play your opponent safe ad infinitum, without ever trying
to pocket anything? In theory, yes, you could—before either player is
committed to solid balls or striped ones. Once that committment is
reached, however, the common rule (in both 8-ball and 9-ball, actually)
is that any player who fails to contact a legal target in three consecutive turns loses the game. It won't happen very often in 8-ball, though,
because with all those balls on the table, even your opponent's unsuc-

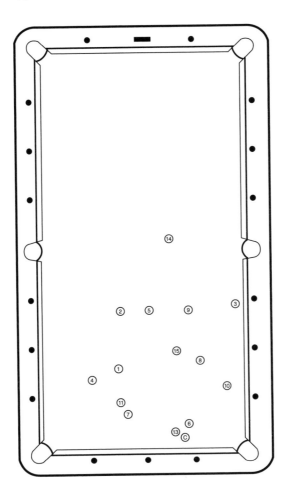

Diagram 85

cessful attempts to hit his object balls first instead of yours are likely to alter the table layout, and the more the balls get spread, the more tricky defense becomes.

Note, however, that when you do go on the offense in 8-ball, all the straight-pool position guidelines apply. Do not move secondary object balls that are already pocketable, after sinking the one you intended; clear paths to the corner pockets for your own balls (not your opponent's); get the balls off the rail early in your sequence; don't use English or the rails unnecessarily; have a safety-valve shot available when you separate clustered balls; and so on.

7

A SMARTER APPROACH TO 9-BALL

In a way, this game is pool's version of Russian roulette; nothing counts except what happens last. It's the game you see the pros playing on cable TV; the reason for that is that 9-ball is the most TV-friendly of all the pool games. It's offense-oriented and extremely fast (it's rare for any single game to last much more than a few minutes). Straight-pool defense can involve excruciatingly long periods where neither player has anything to shoot at; 9-ball defense seldom takes more than two or three turns before an open shot emerges.

Except in its tournament format, 9-ball, like poker and backgammon, is nearly senseless to play except for stakes. That's how the game was originally conceived: whoever legally sinks the 9 collects from everybody else in the game. (Nine-ball is often played as a *ring game*, meaning three to six players can get in on the action. I never heard of a game with more than six players, though. If you missed, you'd be waiting half the night for your next turn.) In many parts of the South, little other pool is played.

Nine-ball is played like its venerable ancestor, "rotation"; that is, the lowest-numbered ball on the table must be contacted first by the cue ball. Once that is accomplished, any object ball falling into a hole, whether intended or not, counts, to the mere extent that the shooter continues his turn. In rotation, you keep score by adding up the points on the balls sunk; whoever totals 61 or more first wins the game (the balls' total value, 1 through 15, is 120; 61 wins because it's one more than half). In 9-ball, however, you make no such calculations. Your only reward for sinking anything but the 9 is that you get another turn. Thus it's entirely possible to make every ball on the table *but* the 9 and thereby lose, and it happens all the time with beginning players; it's most often a classic example of choking under pressure.

To the untrained eye, 9-ball, even as played by top pros, appears to be simplistic and lucky. To win at 8-ball, you must sink the 8 cleanly, as you meant to. No such restriction applies in 9-ball, and when you "slop in" the 9 through dumb luck or any other means, you get paid as though you had done so with consummate skill. Beginning and even intermediate players often do "ride the 9" that way, meaning they sacrifice any reasonable chance at sinking the lowest-numbered ball in favor of driving that ball, or the cue ball, into the 9 and seeing if they can get lucky somehow.

As played by experts, though, 9-ball's only truly and consistently lucky factor is how the balls lie after being blasted open. Occasionally they can luckily roll into position for a very easy runout—cynical players, especially those on the losing end, refer to these situations as *road maps*—but most of the time, 9-ball is a deceptively difficult and complex game of angles. As there is never more than one legal target for you at any time, the three-question process we examined in Chapter 4 becomes more significant than ever in 9-ball. Failure to execute satisfactorily when it comes to the third question (*Where do you want to be on your next shot to get somewhere favorable for the shot after that?*) is commonly called *getting on the wrong side of the ball*, and it usually will require you to revamp your entire position plan.

Nine-ball is also a shotmaker's delight; of all pool games, this is the one where accuracy goes furthest to overcome precision. There is an expert class of players who approach it just that way, not overly concerned about pinpoint position because they have no fear of firing away from anyplace; that approach is most often referred to as a *power game*. When good players go *mano a mano*, certainly you will see finesses such as safeties or hooks; and responses to those moves, which include *kicks* (shots where the cue ball takes on one or more rails before contacting the required ball) and spectacular jump shots, and especially carom shots wherein the cue ball sinks the 9 after meeting the required object ball first. That's why young players take to the game so well; they're able to both pocket the object ball and move their cue ball all over the table, and successful 9-ball is little more than a combination of those two abilities.

I would be remiss, however, if I counseled you to trust your approach to 9-ball to your shotmaking and nothing else. While the game can be played, and well, that way, let's try to build you a better-rounded foundation than your mere eyesight, starting with an analysis of how the balls are racked and broken.

The Break

As you probably know by now, the balls are racked in a diamond-shaped formation for 9-ball, with the 9 in the middle and the 1 up front. The remaining seven object balls can go anyplace. A number of players do put the 2 at the back end of the rack, theorizing that if the breaker does sink something, there will still be distance between the 1 and 2, which should help to slow him down. That reasoning, as we shall soon see, has its fallacies.

There seems to be a definite advantage in breaking from the side, rather than straight-on from the head ball, in 9-ball. In fact, in seniors tournament play (for players age 50 and over), players are barred from breaking that way; they are confined to a break area defined by the square between the outside diamonds on the short rail and the second diamonds on the long rails. Let's say, though, that you and your opponent are not restricted that way. You'd logically do as you do in 8-ball—that is, find the table's "live" areas for breaking, if the first one or two you try do not yield favorable results. But whichever breaking location you eventually settle on, be aware that the break in 9-ball is potentially a much more formidable advantage than in 8-ball, something to remember when making the break part of any handicapped-game proposition.

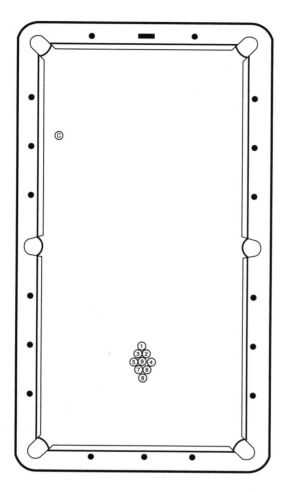

Diagram 86

Equally as important as knowledge of where to place the cue ball, and where to drive it, is an understanding of the potential results. So let's take a closer look at a typical 9-ball rack, and what you might expect, assuming you execute your break stroke correctly.

Suppose, in Diagram 86, you're breaking from the right as you face the racked balls. You're trying for the fullest hit on the 1 you can achieve from your starting position, but that hit will not be quite as simple as it seems because of your added speed. So the exact path of the 1-ball will be determined by where you strike it. If you hit the 1 to the right of its center as you face it, it will move toward the opposite side pocket, precisely what many expert players will try to achieve. If you hit it more toward its center, it will tend to move more toward the bottom corner pocket on the left side. Sometimes, and unpredictably, it can take a path toward the top corner pocket opposite the side where you broke. Thus the 1 can actually be pocketed in any one of three pockets.

The two balls immediately behind the 1 (the 2 and 3 in the diagram) rarely go far. The two balls flanking the 9, the 4 and 5, are the fastest leaving the rack on the break. The flanking ball on the same side you broke is the more likely of the two to visit the nearest corner pocket; most often, both balls will strike the nearest long rails and continue to move. The 9 itself is the least predictable ball in the rack; it generally moves forward and slowly, and occasionally will reach the bottom corner opposite the side from which the break was executed (but that's no better than a 1-in-10 proposition, even when the best players get it on). When the 9 does fall on the break for a lucky outright win, most often it's bopped in by another wildly careening object ball.

The two balls directly behind the 9 aren't much better travelers than the two directly in front of it. The tail ball in the rack (the 8 in the diagram) is the third-fastest ball leaving the rack, and could travel all the way uptable to score in a far corner pocket.

The ball racked where you see the 5 is the most commonly pocketed ball when breaking from where the cue ball lies in the diagram. Second most frequently pocketed is the 1, usually in the side pocket opposite the side from which the balls were broken, and this ball really represents the breaker's only control (and it's partial, at best) over the outcome of his break. The third most likely ball to fall will be the back ball, most often into the corner pocket nearest where the cue ball began.

Most balls falling on a 9-ball break go directly into pockets, as just described. Other shots made on the break are due to collisions between object balls, most often involving the fastest-moving ones (those flanking the 9, and the tail ball). But those are lucky collisions, depending on infinitesimal differences in timing and pathways, virtually totally unpredictable.

As in 8-ball, you should strive for a break in which the cue ball dies in the middle of the table. This increases the possibility of your having an open shot at the 1, should it not go in on your break while something else does. Even if the 1 should fall, center table will, most of the time, afford you the best starting place, even though no options exist as to what ball you must begin with.

So much for the 9-ball rack. The best advice I can give you concerning the dismantling of that rack is similar to what was advised for 8-ball: utilize all the speed you can *control*, rather than all you can produce. What you don't want is the cue ball traveling madly all around the table at the same time all those object balls are in flight.

Thinking Ahead

It certainly can't hurt to revisit the big three questions of position play, with the proviso that 9-ball alters them slightly by its very nature. It's no longer a question of which ball you'd *like* to shoot next, after the task immediately at hand, but rather which one you *have* to, since you must proceed in numerical rotation. So:

a. Which ball must you shoot next, after the one you're aiming at now?

b. Which ball comes after that?

c. Where, or at least on which side of the ball identified in (a) do you want to be to get somewhere favorable for the ball of (b)?

As the game never offers you more than one legal target at a time, it becomes more critical than ever to get on the right side of the ball in position play. If, for instance, you determine that the 4-ball should be cut to its left for optimal position on the 5, and your cue ball winds up somewhere where the 4 can still be made but only by cutting it to its right instead, obviously you'll need to revamp your overall position plan—if it can be recouped at all. Ending up on the wrong side of an object ball is one of 9-ball's most universal bugaboos, even among experts.

There's another aspect to thinking ahead in 9-ball, though, and while it represents a fairly advanced plane, it's worth looking at. It's the table layout that includes miniclusters of unpocketable balls. Say, for instance, that the 5 and 6 have one another tied up. Even if you have open shots on all the remaining balls preceding the 5, you still need a plan for sending your cue ball from one of those object balls to open up the 5 and 6. And it gets even stickier than that: if you *don't* have open shots on one or more of the balls preceding the 5, and you need to play defense somehow, you will be leaving your opponent at very little risk—*unless* your safety plan also deals with the troublesome 5-6. Still with me? Suppose you successfully hide the 3-ball on your opponent. Why should he even try to hit it, when by missing it he suffers nothing more than giving you ball in hand and that 5-6 still to deal with? Unless you've got a damn good defensive plan for taking on the 5-6 when you come to it, you'll simply be solving his problem for him. Accordingly, try to combine your defensive plays with tactics that separate trouble balls at the same time, so your opponent is definitely at risk if he doesn't respond to your safety. (In the example just given, you'd correctly look for a way to drive the 3 into the 5-6 while hiding it from your opponent at the same time. That way, his failure to contact the 3 would put him in hot water, as it's supposed to.)

As in 8-ball, don't begin firing in open balls just because they're there and seem obvious. Look beyond the obvious, and formulate a plan that takes in all the balls, not just the one directly before you. Don't wait till you come to a trouble spot to deal with that trouble spot. It won't serve you any better in pool than it does in life.

Untrapping Yourself

We could have examined the critical technique of responding to your opponent's defense in the 8-ball section, too. But the fact is, situations

in which your cue ball is hidden from direct view of a legal target
come up much more often in 9-ball than in 8-ball, for two reasons: 9-
ball offers you only one legal target at a time, and a far higher percentage of 9-ball players have a generally correct view of their game
than 8-ballers do.

The formal name for this situation is *snookered*, from the game of
that name; in pool, it's almost as commonly called *hooked*. By any
name, though, it potentially represents the imminent loss of the game,
if your opponent is capable (unless, as we've just seen, problem areas
exist in your layout in addition to the one you face). So let's consider
how you might respond to being hooked besides in blind panic.

First of all, consider the overall table layout. As we've just seen, if
there are other problem areas elsewhere, you're not under quite the
same pressure to complete a legal hit (although your opponent could try
to hook you right back; your failing to make a legal hit in three consecutive turns costs you the game, too). If all the balls are open, however, and missing the requisite object ball carries considerable risk,
there are two scenarios to ponder:

1. Can you complete a successful hit somehow? Some 9-ball traps are
simply inescapable, either because of too many balls directly in the
way, or balls that hinder the cue ball's natural path off rails, or both.
When you're up against it like this, do *not* attempt the hope-against-
hope kick; you are then relying on nothing but your opponent's mess-
ing up somehow. Instead, try rolling the closest object ball into the
next-closest one so they interfere with one another's paths to a pocket.
It takes a good touch to bring this off, but at least you're doing something to stay in the game. If you're hooked that badly and the 9 is anywhere near a pocket, pass up the above move in favor of illegally
pocketing the 9. It's a very weak move—your opponent still gets cue
ball-in-hand, with the 9 merely respotted—but it's still better than giving him a gift combination shot early in the game.

2. If the hidden object ball is indeed hittable with a kick, meaning the
cue-ball rail paths you need are clear, now you know why I recom-

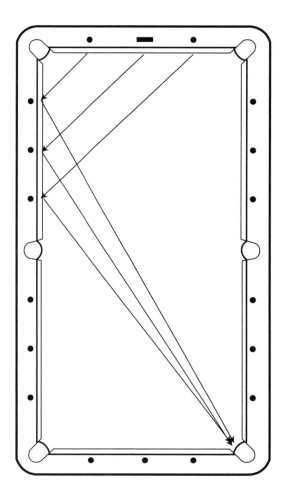

Diagram 87

mended back in the straight-pool chapter that you initiate your bank-shot education by banking the cue ball alone. By now you should have some capacity for visually bisecting the angle, if a one-rail route is indeed available, and that's where the fundamentals of kicking begin.

The other kicking principle you should embrace now is the natural diagonal-paths-to-a-corner-pocket shown in Diagram 87. Depending on the type and condition of the rails and cloth where you play, you may need a tad of favoring English (left-hand as diagrammed) to create these paths, but they are valid, and so are paths parallel to them.

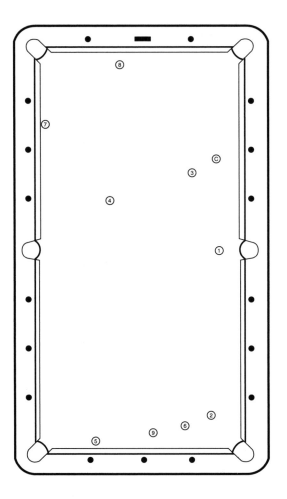

Diagram 88

Now, with that information, it follows that by beginning at the short rail's first diamond and aiming somewhere beyond the long rail's first diamond, you can send your cue ball to a point on the far short rail instead of the corner. If you aim at a point on the long rail short of the first diamond, your cue ball will take a diagonal path short of the opposite corner, and so on. Your results will also vary as more English (and, much more rarely, reverse English) is introduced to the shot.

There is really no substitute for practicing this exercise with a cue ball and an object ball. See how many times in a row you can make contact with various one-rail and two-rail routes. Add cue-ball English,

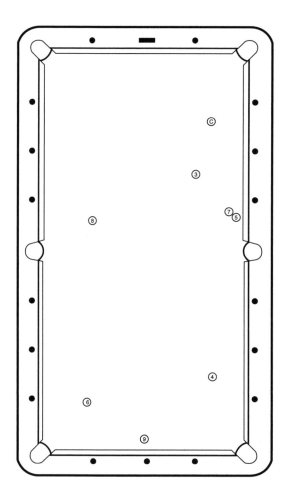

Diagram 89

and when you're comfortable with your progress, try making contact with one side of the object ball or the other. This exercise may sound tedious, but it's invaluable experience for 9-ball since kicking is largely a matter of judgment. (It will also help your 8-ball game in case your opponent has read this, too, and is playing defense on you.)

Playing the Game

Now that we've taken a look at the rudiments of 9-ball offense and defense, let's apply that knowledge to two realistic playing situations, one where the game is available to be run out just as the balls lie, and one where a runout is simply not possible. Diagram 88 shows you exactly what to look for after the break: a logical open pocket for every object ball, and plenty of space between all the balls to work with. Try to achieve a cue-ball location on the 2 that will permit you to avoid the 6 and 9 (no running into already-pocketable balls, remember). You should probably play position on the 4 in that back-corner pocket nearest the 7 and 8, because that's the simplest shot coming off the 3. Draw the cue ball back from the 4 only as far as the line between the second diamonds on the long rails for efficient position on the 5.

The layout of Diagram 89, however, is without future. There is no open pocket for the 3, and even if there were, what would you do with that nasty 5-7 tangle on the near rail? This is an example of the aggressive defense we talked about a few paragraphs ago: drive the 3 downtable and into the interfering 6 (that will ensure the 3 stays down there), at the same time nudging the 5 and 7 apart with the cue ball as you hide the cue ball behind them. Now your opponent has a real problem. If he doesn't overcome your snooker, you're a threat to run out the game, as there is nothing left to stymie you. Remember, the objective of correct defensive play in 9-ball is not simply to stop your opponent, but to directly enhance your chances of winning.

WHAT ARE YOU WAITING FOR? GO BEAT ON PEOPLE

Thank you for your patience and diligence in staying with me through all this. I've put enough information together here that your assimilating it all will unquestionably be an ambitious task. That's why I suggested, back in the early pages, that you take this a bit at a time.

Still, if you're as good at applying what you might have learned from my book as you've been about reading it, your game should be much better for it and you ought to have a whopping jump on your peers. We've visited some instructional areas that have seldom if ever been touched upon by the game's bibliography. Does that mean that it's eccentric or lunatic-fringe? Not even close.

What we've really done is go into greater detail on many concepts that have already been taught. Why haven't the game's previous authors examined the same materials in the same depth? I can't speak for anyone else, but it is possible that they simply didn't think there were enough prospects who wanted to learn pool beyond the customary recreational-fun level. (When I was writing my first book on advanced pool, I was contacted by a quite-visible billiards-industry authority who advised me not to bother; in his opinion, out of the entire pool-playing universe, not 1 player in 20 could make five balls consecutively!)

It would really be a heartbreak if my fellow authors were proven right. Today we have more people at least dabbling in the game than ever before, by far; today's top-of-the-line equipment, especially the cues, is uniformly excellent; and with the currently healthy economy, people generally have more leisure time and money to spend on that time. And this is, in my view, the greatest game known to man with which to fill that time. Yes, the stigmas attached to it ever since the Depression are still around, reinforced on a near-weekly basis by tv and the movies; and I won't attempt to primly deny that such conditions do exist, here and there. But you don't have to come in contact with any of that—in fact, pool's negatives should be extremely easy to avoid— and once you get past all that, the game itself, especially beyond the beginner's level, is just magical.

Although pool affords me an avocational income, I believe that it is I who am in its debt. The game has allowed me to fill literally thousands of hours that would have otherwise been empty; make some dear friends whom I would not even have met otherwise; play in a distinguished New York club with Mark Twain's personal cue on the wall and one of the legends of my business in the audience. (In that game, against a very good player who opened with a run of 50, I ran 75 and 25 back-to-back for a two-inning victory, world-class by any standards and perhaps six levels above my normal speed. Sometimes you just rise to the occasion, or you bring out the best in the game instead of the customary other way around. It really doesn't matter which.)

The way I hope to repay my debt to the game is to help more people play it well, thus keeping it healthy just as with any other individual sport. So go kick some butt, in a friendly way. If I should find my way to your local room—and I do get around—please introduce yourself and ask me to play. We've been through a lot together.